GH
SHIP

Although the subtitle of France-Williams' new book is 'Institutional Racism and the Church of England,' make no mistake: here is a powerful and provocative word to people on both sides of the ocean, wherever racial injustice is found. It's impossible to turn the pages of *Ghost Ship* and not find yourself challenged to turn the nightmare around us into God's dream of a better world.

The Most Rev. Michael B. Curry, Presiding Bishop of The Episcopal Church

France-Williams employs a formidable range of approaches – among them testimony, academic categories, careful research, interviews, anecdote, poetry, humour, parody, exegesis and close reading – to mount a compelling and urgent argument for the church's institutional and personal failure to receive the gift the Holy Spirit in the lives, bodies and callings of its BAME witnesses. Most of all he models prophetic ministry: pleading, portraying, persuading and ultimately inspiring the church that has caused so much hurt and grief but that despite all he still bravely loves. This is a testament of truth; and an epistle of power.

Revd Dr Sam Wells, Vicar of St Martin in the Fields

Ghost Ship is poetically, formally and spiritually courageous. The profound honesty with which it is written is matched only by the honesty it asks for. The power of that honesty offers wondrous scope for the liberation and revitalisation of the Anglican church.

Kobna Holdbrook-Smith

Ghost Ship has been many years in the making and I have been honoured to have journeyed with the author as his prophetic vision has developed and matured, culminating in this book. This text is an excellent combination of historical analysis, personal reflection, poetry, biblical hermeneutics and first hand narratives, all combined to produce a highly readable book. Its key strength is that it is written by an insider, one whose love for the Church of England is such, that he is willing to tell her the truth!

Anthony Reddie, Director of the Oxford Centre for Religion and Culture, University of Oxford

Racism thrives best in the company of silence. That's why *Ghost Ship* is such an important book. Azariah France-Williams' voice from within provokes a long overdue, honest conversation around how we recognise and dismantle the deep rooted racist attitudes and systems that still haunt the Church from our colonial past. If we are to play our full God-given role in de-escalating racial tension and in building a society where no one is disadvantaged because of the colour of their skin, we cannot afford to ignore this book and its message. You don't have to be black or brown to call out racism – but you have to be complicit with it not to!

Revd Steve Chalke, Founder and Leader, Oasis Global

Searing, truthful, devastating, prophetic. I hope this book reaches a wide and worldwide audience. And for those of us who are white Anglicans, it should cause us to weep in recognition of our complicity. Then resolve to be part of the change that must come.

Lucy Winkett, Rector of St James' Church, Piccadilly

In this powerful book, France-Williams tells the stories of discrimination many of us review in our heads on the way home after work and put aside to be cheerful and present with people we love, and then we go back the next morning. For those of us who have committed our lives to the service of God through the Anglican Church, the institutional weight of slavery and colonialism and their legacy of racism bear down daily, whether we have decided to cope like a raging and blinded Samson in the temple of Dagon or a smiling token carefully packaged. France-Williams digs it all up and puts it on the page. Ouch! But, thankfully, he reframes the isolating burden of discrimination as institutional racism, the presenting sin of the church. With that sin has come the great potential for repentance, deep institutional transformation, and the salvation of a radical change of course. Let us take it up in our time.

Winnie Varghese, Trinity Church Wall Street, New York

In *Ghost Ship*, France-Williams takes on white supremacy in the Church of England and the Anglican Communion with precision, imagination, and confidence. Every page is evidence of his ability to make complex matters accessible to neophytes and experts alike. It is within reason to expect this tome to become a standard in the training of church leaders, lay and ordained. His exploration of Pan-African Anglicanism is a gift to students of church history and shows that he stands on the shoulders of faithful giants. I commend this book to a world desperately in need of France-Williams's pioneering imagination and insight.

The Rev. Canon Broderick Greer, Writer and Episcopal Priest

This is a powerful book. Its power comes not in loud or angry protest, but in prophetic storytelling that speaks truth to power, reflecting back on the Church its failings when it comes to racial justice. In an understated way, it combines personal testimony with imagery, real-life accounts and a range of voices who put together a mosaic of centuries-long racial injustice in the Church. The at times devastating critique of the status quo within the Church is not dampened by the beautiful writing, but calls the reader to attention. It is a lament of the state of the Church and a rallying call towards a better way.

Chine McDonald, writer and broadcaster

Intelligence and passion fuel Azariah France-Williams' dissection of the leadership 'club' – people like me – at the heart of the Church of England's failure to own and address its racism. The reader need not accept all his arguments uncritically, to recognise this authentic black voice needs to be heard.

The Right Reverend Dr David Walker, Bishop of Manchester

GHOST SHIP

*Institutional Racism and
the Church of England*

A. D. A. France-Williams

scm press

© A. D. A. France-Williams 2020

Published in 2020 by SCM Press
Editorial office
3rd Floor, Invicta House,
108–114 Golden Lane,
London EC1Y 0TG, UK

www.scmpress.co.uk

SCM Press is an imprint of Hymns Ancient & Modern Ltd
(a registered charity)

Hymns Ancient & Modern® is a registered trademark of
Hymns Ancient & Modern Ltd
13A Hellesdon Park Road, Norwich,
Norfolk NR6 5DR, UK

British Library Cataloguing in Publication data
A catalogue record for this book is available
from the British Library

978-0-334-05935-6

Typeset by Regent Typesetting
Printed and bound by
CPI Group (UK) Ltd

To the 230 people who died from
drowning when the M.V. *Christena* ferry
sank on 1 August 1970 between the
federation Islands of St Kitts and Nevis.
It was the celebration of emancipation day.

May they...

Rest in Power.

Contents

By the rivers of Babylon, there we sat down, yea, we wept, when we remembered Zion.

We hanged our harps upon the willows in the midst thereof.

For there they that carried us away captive required of us a song; and they that wasted us required of us mirth, saying, Sing us one of the songs of Zion.

How shall we sing the Lord's song in a strange land? (Ps. 137.1–4)

Acknowledgements

To my publishing team at SCM Press. They have been a huge support throughout the entire process of writing. David and Nicola in particular have dared me to be bold, and cautioned me to be wise. I was fortunate to have been based in a conscious and compassionate church while I wrote this book. The Parochial Church Council supported my request to write one day a week, and my having a month's sabbatical to complete my first draft. My clergy colleagues stepped in to ensure the work and worship of the church continued while I conducted my research.

At times this book is a solo effort, and other times there are a chorus of voices. They are Team Ten, people who love Jesus, love justice, and a number who love the Book of Common Prayer. They are ten members of the Church of England, women and men, brown and black, who took the risk of trusting me with their stories as a way of demonstrating how institutional racism operates. I was told other stories that for legal reasons cannot be featured here. I commend the bravery of those who confided in me, and pray for good resolutions and healing from the abuses of power they have experienced.

I want to acknowledge the many of you who responded to my invitation for an interview about the Church of England. Some of you I travelled to, others of you came to me, and some of you were Skyped in from overseas. You were all candid and courageous. While not all of your words made the pages, all of your thoughts made the book. So heartfelt gratitude to Glynne, Dean, Elizabeth, Tunde, Hannah, David, Winnie, Margaret, Amos, Kamil, Adrian, Rose, Chine, Bob, Keon, Harold, Camille and Eve.

Now I turn to the people who gave of their time, skill and love to help me tend the garden of this book. Whether you were brown, white or black, you all had green fingers. You people shovelled on fertiliser, squirted weed-killer, and helped me dig deeper, enabling the young garden to take shape. You cleared the overgrowth, creating a path for the sojourners of these accounts to travel well. I recognise Eliana, Richard, Laura, Anthony, Lucy, Stephen, Dulcie, Liz, Hannah, Micah, Paul, Steve, Selina, Kit, Grant, Julia, Kate, Olivia, Denis, Andre, Ann, Rafael, Mary, Debbie, Martin, Naomi, Graham, Ursula, Tim, Juliette, David, Natasha, Gus, Sharon, Tony, Elysia, Jayme, Darius, Anna, Elizabeth, Karen, Eve, Joel, Jonathan, Robert and Elvira.

I have had the absolute honour of being a member of three small groups of predominantly people of colour. One is made up of clergy, the other of professionals, and the third is family. These relationships have been a source of solace and support. To share a meal without feeling the need to repress one's broader heritage is 'peng'. These groups have acted as both a nest I could fly from, and a nest I could fall into. Sisters, daughters, brothers, mothers, fathers and sons. They have gathered round, knowing at times I needed quiet, knowing when to share a laugh, and knowing when to hold me when the tears fell.

Who's Who and What's What

The Audience

There are a number of readers and listeners I am envisaging. One demographic is people of colour whose stories have been those of the eccentric. That is, those on the edge of the circle who swing towards and then away from a centre-point. Those whose recorded stories too often orbit a white male sun which is a centre-point of a shared known universe. If we were describing a slave ship, these would be the enslaved women, men and children whose existence appears to be predicated on the whims and wishes of the predators.

Second, I am appealing to those in high office in the English church and society. Those for whom factors like college, cricket, class and context have conferred a set of interlocking advantages known as 'white privilege'. Should this be a slave ship we were delineating, this group could be the ship's captains and the boat owners (who privately captain the captains). No matter the benevolence of the captain, the brutality inscribed in the ship's design compromises the power of the captain to be good. The compression and oppression of the ship's materials and design warp even the straightest arrow – meaning the targets can never be hit, the arrow always travels wide of the mark.

The third group are those who work for national institutions like education, the National Health Service, the prison service, the armed forces, the British civil service, the Church of England, or the press. These are people who work within a predetermined framework. They are of good heart but are tasked with near impossible demands, with limited budgets, and ultimately asked to keep their institution alive. This is in order to heighten the perception that the institution is a going concern, and to lessen the concern that it is just going. This stratum of workers is drawn from the working and middle classes. On board a seafaring vessel they would form the crew members, those who are not the elite, but who have a level of agency through association with being the accepted normal, the unquestioned status quo. Again, whiteness offers an umbrella under which members can find shelter. Any valid and/or valuable connection with those by whom they are employed to engage or volunteer to serve is circumscribed by the captain's whims and the boat owner's wishes.

Fourth, the interested public – who I find to be somewhere on the scale between 'agnostic apathetic' and 'abolitionist activist' when conversations around race and the Church of England arise. During the period of the abolition of the transatlantic slave trade in the UK, white politicians, artists, journalists, activists, academics, clergy, Quakers, scientists, and others began to reassess their conditioned narratives. They began to seek out the voices and views of the emancipated, and reported on the conditions of those still in chains. May this book play its part in the liberation of our collective imagination to be a church enacting justice within its community, training the clergy in colleges to build better ships where all can find safety and safe passage.[1]

ABC

Shorthand for the Archbishop of Canterbury. ABCs are like Doctor Who. They are usually white men championing things white men like to champion, and one day there will be a white woman who will broaden the scope and we will all celebrate, though many will think it controversial. But no one can imagine a black or brown ABC. It is not as easy as 'one, two, three' in this case, whatever the Jackson 5 may claim. Several incarnations of ABC will be referenced here, primarily from the last 30 years. Spoiler alert: the report card conclusion is largely 'Could do better.'

Harold Lewis

A black historian who knows the church and has documented and helped instigate many good things. He was head of the Office for Black Ministries in the Episcopalian Church in America. Episcopalian is an alternative term for Anglican. He met with and inspired Barry Thorley (he is coming up ...), he hosted Glynne Gordon-Carter and inspired her work, and organised for African Americans to sponsor black Anglicans who could not get support from the UK branch.

Wilfred Wood

A black West Indian with fire shut up in his bones. In other words, he is passionate, playful and prophetic. He has been a literary companion through this process. The stories I heard about him, the boldness of his challenge to the Church of England hierarchy, but more importantly his role within the black community, are nothing short of monumental. He was the first black bishop in the Church of England in 1985.[2]

Elizabeth Henry

A bit like 'Storm' from *X-Men*. She valiantly led (until May 2020) the inclusion push on behalf of black and brown Anglicans – storming the citadel, inspiring the wounded and the weakened to get up and keep fighting. Blood, sweat and tears, black and proud, and she is a northerner. She'd call for a Truth and Reconciliation process here to document the ass-whupping many black and brown clergy have suffered under a seemingly inviolable white power structure.

Glynne Gordon-Carter

She is a boss. She began the inclusion push in the late 1980s and built the foundations that Elizabeth builds on now. Against all the odds, at lower pay to her peers, she thought globally and acted locally. She is a figure of folklore. She wrote an amazing book which documented the 'slings and arrows of outrageous fortune'. The 'committee' she led suffered in the pursuit of racial justice, and like Hamlet they had to decide whether to continue living, or not.

The Cross and the Crown (Club)

This is my name for the General Synod, the governing body of the Church of England. We are proudly, hubristically even, the National Church, the Established Church. The Cross is a demonstration of uncoercive love. A church with the cross at centre shows a heart and wallet commitment to those on the edges of society. It begins with the poor realising it too is improvised, and together new realities can emerge from the chaos. A church with the crown at the centre puts its power behind the rich, the patrons, the good and great of a society. The type of church that is the good and great of society. The way of the crown implicitly holds to a world of order and control, a hierarchy that admits no dissent. The Church of England is both the Cross and the Crown, but it is also a (Club), and it is the (Club) management that seeks to dictate the terms and conditions (the brackets indicate it is slightly obscured).

Reggie and Ronnie (not the Kray twins, but similar)

Reggie and Ronnie are the Church of England's bouncers and butchers, the gatekeepers and guardians, the mortal enemies of people like Wilfred and Glynne, and now Elizabeth. They embody the spirit of 'not in my backyardism', which is the knee-jerk, and just jerk, response to so much innovation, life and energy, youth and vitality on offer. The fear of everything being covered in Jerk sauce prevents the Church of England's purists and puritans from countenancing any other way but their way.

Aslan

We know of Aslan, the lion of legend, through C. S. Lewis's Chronicles of Narnia books. Aslan is alone. Within hurting communities, Aslan's roar goes unheeded. Within colleges where Church of England clergy are trained, Aslan's is a cry of lament for the 'hazing' that occurs for many black and brown students. There is the impotence of white power structures to challenge these practices. It is not just about developing a supportive stance with black and brown students, but also taking a stance of radical advocacy among the rest of the white fraternity, unequivocally demonstrating that this is everybody's problem and is everybody's business. Aslan is also seeking to breathe warm life into our congregations that are frozen in time and frozen in place. But Aslan is too often locked out of church fêtes, worship rehearsals, and our vestries.

Jadis

The bringer of winter. She is usually accompanied by a pack of white wolves. There is a weather condition called whiteness. If you live in the arctic and have the right clothing and access to warmth, you are good to go and explore. It is a different type of expedition if you're exposed and denied access to the resources necessary to your survival, let alone your flourishing. People of colour in England live in a system maladapted for their wellbeing, whether education, health, housing, justice, or religion. Jadis has frozen our institutions. Jadis has petrified many a white consciousness. James Cone, speaking of his own context, said: 'White theologians, not having felt the sting of oppression, will find it most difficult to criticise this nation, for the condemnation of America means a condemnation of self.'[3]

Fedora Hat Man

This guy was fated to take the punishment Reggie and Ronnie wanted to dole out. This guy represents Windrush, which I see as a symbol of all who travel here looking for a better life. Fedora Hat Man and Woman come here to serve and lead within the mother country. Our current ABC quotes Samuel Smiles' comment on the welcome the Huguenot refugees received when escaping from France. He documents 'The large and liberal spirit of the English church, and the glorious asylum which England has in all times given to foreigners flying for refuge against oppression and tyranny.'[4] Sadly, Fedora Hat Man has not known that story, but rather came willingly and has become internally displaced and oppressed within the place he once thought home.

Second Fedora Hat Man

The sort of black and brown person Ronnie and Reggie can do business with, cowed and subservient. Ronnie and Reggie have taken a cosh to them, and the internalisation of trauma ensures they submit and keep coming back for more pain.

Ade the Griot

A storyteller who creates stories and recreates history, from a long line of the Griot who are West African poets and story-tellers. Her full name is Adetokunbo and it means 'the crown came from over the sea'.[5]

BraveSlave

I can neither confirm nor deny that BraveSlave is an alter-ego and avatar to enable the author to say with force what he sees, hears and feels through story and poetry.

Notes

1 Rediker, M. (2007), *The Slave Ship*, London: John Murray, p. 7. Rediker outlines a set of interlocking relationships that simultaneously made the slave ship operate and eventually ended the trade. I have based my list on his.

2 By 'black' I am using the term in the way that black thinker, theologian and polemicist, the mighty James Cone, RIP, uses it. He said: 'the true black thinker is in a different position. He (old-school male pronoun alert) cannot be black and be identified with the powers that be ... when one stands where the black man stands, a creature who has visions of a future because the present is unbearable. And the black man will cling to the future as a means of passionately rejecting the present' (Cone, J. (1970), *A Black Theology of Liberation*, Philadelphia: Lippincott, p. 49).

3 Ibid.

4 Welby, J. (2018), *Reimagining Britain*, London: Bloomsbury, p. 199.

5 www.behindthename.com/names/usage/western-african.

Prologue
Tears and Troubadours:
A Tale by Ade the Griot

The kingdom was for all. The queen was the architect of fair and flourishing lands. She was loved by all and she had a penchant for singing, which was known across her kingdom. She would sing her laws, she would sing her commands, she would sing of her love for all her people in the many lands in which she ruled. One fine day a messenger arrived at court with a request for the queen to visit a far-off part of her kingdom where she was required to broker a reconciliation between troubled clans. All had been tried and it was felt she alone could catalyse the process of peace. The messenger urged her to make haste and leave in a few short days. After some deliberation she decided to go. But what to do about the rule here? She had a wise community of elders and children who were beyond interest in the binaries of rulers and subjects, us and them. They would not promote themselves, and she would not pressure them. She determined to entrust her other subjects with the task. She planned to hold a banquet with the heads of all the tribes and clans of the people. She would instigate a council and the various clans would be encouraged to share the rule as first among equals.

The day before the banquet, a delegation of one of the clans sought an audience with the queen. Their spokesperson implored her that they were her most capable and able stewards, they were certainly her most eager. She was not convinced, but nevertheless decided to exercise faith in them. The queen was persuaded to allow them to take the lead first. They scurried around in giddy delight and misheard her instructions, which were to share the responsibility of forming society with all who were part of it. They were told to hold the banquet in her absence, and to collectively decide the sequence of who would next have the honour of rule, and who would be next after that. The queen sang her charge. 'All were to create society, and all were to benefit from it.' This is what the queen sang. They were to be the first clan among equals.

However, the first clan reinterpreted this as: share the rule among yourselves, on behalf of the others. They heard this was their gift, their burden, until the queen's return. They told themselves this version of events so often they began to believe it was what the queen had actually sung. The queen's discomfort grew seeing their obvious perverse pleasure, but she had to begin the journey, the messenger was quite insistent. She wrote some letters before leaving and had them secretly distributed to her wise community of elders and children who were scattered about the kingdom. Her message was that they were to gather should a problem emerge. She departed for her travels. No sooner had she gone than the castle and surrounding town were occupied by the clan who took the rule. They had a lot of luggage and appeared to be coming to stay, not just visit. The banquet was held later that evening but when the other leaders of the clans and tribes arrived, the spokesperson from the first clan met them in the courtyard between the castle's entrance and first gate. He apologised that there was only enough for the first clan. This was not true. Furthermore he sent the other leaders home to await another banquet date. He walked them outside the first gate and away from the courtyard and the castle. He went back in and the gate was closed and locked. It had never been locked before. Some accepted this concession and returned without argument, trusting the queen's delegated authority. The proud chiefs, sages and tribal leaders felt the anger of the slight, and the underlying sense of injustice. Before they left, they stationed themselves outside the first gate singing the song of the queen in defiance at this turn of events.

The invitation to another banquet never came. The true

sovereign was remembered in words, but no longer in deeds, her portraits were taken down from the walls. The broad kingdom was neglected and its subjects grew disillusioned by their pain. In the castle, the occupying clan began to think of the castle and grounds as the kingdom entire. They began to call themselves 'the first and the last clan', among themselves. Eventually the maps were redrawn in order to focus resources on the new, narrow, castle kingdom. They installed a dungeon for those from the outside who tried to penetrate the defences looking for the old maps. The forgotten places that had been drawn out would not go quietly into the night. They took to lighting fires, desiring recognition, and some in desperation turned to self-immolation. Such was the desire to be seen – if only briefly – by those in the town and the castle, as they flickered away to embers and dust.

The stewards of the narrow kingdom heard of this new form of protest. They resented the distraction from the life they were crafting for themselves. The fires of the forgotten places began to cause noxious fumes, and the blazes were lasting longer and getting closer to the town surrounding the castle. One was chosen from the group of stewards to be the king to consolidate rule. One of his first acts was to establish a guard, and his second was to begin erecting a wall outside the surrounding town. The queen was spoken about less and less often, until people began to forget she had even existed. No one could recall her face, her voice, or her bearing. People no longer sang. The melodies had faded, only some snippets were recalled in dreams, which evaporated on waking.

In the forgotten places the wise women, men and children gathered according to the queen's wishes. They were scholars, magicians, jesters and storytellers who committed themselves to each other and to the cause of justice and peace. They began to meet regularly in secret to determine how to uproot the tangled and deep causes of the trauma experienced in the for-gotten places. They pondered whether the ancient maps could be restored to include all the kingdom and unblock the narrow kingdom's grip on power. They often met around a pint of ale with sympathetic innkeepers where they could converse freely without fear of discovery. During one such gathering there was a knock on the door. They were terrified, fearing trouble. But then they heard the sweetest sound. Music of the old days floated through the windows. The music came from a mixed group of travelling troubadours, smelly, tatty, but joyful, who descended on them. This group knew fragments of the old songs, which they played. Some of the men of the group even began to sing sections of the old songs in strong tenor voices, and a flame of hope was lit. Night after night, larger and larger groups gathered together in secret, singing, laughing, making merry, arguing, plotting, praying, and making love, until sleep would conquer their reverie and they snuck back to their homes and settlements. Ten days after the troubadours had arrived, an idea struck the people. It would take a couple of days to arrange, but the plan was that the travelling troupe would seek entrance into the narrow kingdom. They would offer their services as entertainers, and once inside they would find a way to redraw the maps, redistribute the wealth, and restore the honour of the true sovereign.

A couple of days later, a great procession of the forgotten people marched on the castle led by three chosen musicians of the troubadour band, one woman, a fine musician, with two men either side of her. When the castle doors were opened the newly appointed king surveyed the scene. He was disconcerted by the silent masses staring and starving. One of the young men stepped forward and unrolled a scroll, he spoke up declaring they were there to offer services to the new king and the whole kingdom. They would play and compose music for all to enjoy and all to play a part in creating a new society. They would be the bridge between the worlds.

The king initially rebuffed the suggestion, claiming they already had musicians at court and did not need any more. He turned on his heels. But the crowd began to boo. The king's guards flooded through the gates. This was a shock. The broad kingdom had not seen guards before, as conflicts had always been resolved without recourse to violence or threat. The company of wise people began to despair, but they stood their ground. Some guards stood around the king as the unrest mounted. The guards and king shuffled backwards as the gate began to close. The crowd as one began to surge forwards. Quick as a flash, the female troubadour began to play her pipe, softly at first, but loud enough to quell the clamour. Then she played with vigour as people began to sway and clap, her two companions produced a tabor drum and a small lute and accompanied her in the, at times haunting, at times happy, tune. As the air cleared, the king dismissed his personal guard, and appeared to be moved by the music, as he stood in the gap in the gate with a small retinue of stewards. They all saw how mesmerised the crowd had become. She had a power to becalm people. The king suffered bad dreams, and wanted her. The king waited for the end of the song and invited the woman to step forward and moved to the side to allow her to pass through the first gate into the castle courtyard. The crowd cheered as the king ushered her in with a broad grin and a wave to the now placated subjects.

The other musicians followed behind along with some of the wise company. The gate was closed and the crowds began to make their way home, excited to learn what changes would now occur. The king waited for a few moments then his smile dropped like a discarded mask. He nodded and a burly guard laden with a heavy chain grabbed the woman and began to bind her and drag her towards to the king. The two young men sought to prevent her being dragged off in such a manner. Other guards marched into position and when the young men did not stop they suffered a vicious beating. A few of the older members of the wise company moved forward with the woman. They were so frail they were left unchallenged. When the show of strength was ended the woman stood bound, the men convulsing on the floor from their punishment, and the frail company of the wise looked on in horror.

The king looked at the woman for a long time, he caressed her cheek with the back of his hand, grazing her cheek with his signet ring. She was silent and did not resist. An older woman, a member of the company straightened her bent back and spoke up:

'Oh king, take her not as your slave but as your seer, provide for her needs, and heed her advice, she can be the bridge to the wider ancient kingdom of the lost queen. She can be a bridge using music as her companion had said.'

At the mention of the queen the king balked: 'There is no queen! That is just a myth for the ignorant, and the demented. We built all this. Be gone old hag, or you too will be bound.'

At that the gate was opened a crack, just enough for the elders and two male musicians to be unceremoniously shoved outside. The king had the woman assigned to the dungeons. He would send for her when he suffered in his sleep, and when he had visitors to the kingdom. He would have her play the pipe, though it was always mournful, a doleful heavy sound. No amount of threat, or actual violence, could persuade her to lead them in a merry jig; so in the end he gave up and left her to play her lament, which was beautiful in its own way.

The woman grew thin and weak. She was again brought before a delegation from afar. She was handed her pipe and ordered to play, but the head of this delegation said: 'No, I will hear her sing.' She had not been asked to sing before, and she paused, looking to the king who nodded his approval. The woman with tears in her eyes began to sing and the hall grew still. Where had they heard that voice before?

She looked straight at them, her eyes piercing the facade. Her moist eyes held a gentle nobility the court had not noticed, or had ignored until this moment. She stood up, shoulders rolled back. Her voice was the voice of the queen, her face the forgotten face of the queen, her bearing that of the queen. She sang:

I left you, to see you reflect me,
you became less than true,
and less than free,
my freedom song trampled in dust,
our people now broken and crushed,
I thought if I came as one of the people,
you would find a way to see us as equal,
I came vulnerable, as a loving friend,
but evil exists here, but its dominion will end,
my song will be taught far and wide,

though here my song cannot abide,
but my melody will never be finished,
this flame of hope, never extinguished.

The king rose, upending the table in a frenzied rage and rushed towards the singing queen, knocking her to the ground. His guards held her fast, and the king gagged her, but could not look into her eyes, which held no emotion but sorrow. She was sent back to the cold, dark dungeon. Word got out that the woman was enslaved and the broad kingdom lost hope; her true identity was covered up. The remaining troubadours left the broad kingdom to spread her music where it could be learned. The wise company grew old, tired, and died leaving a few half-filled journals of their ambitions for the kingdom before it was taken over. The narrow kingdom simply became known as 'the kingdom'. The song was rumoured to have reached far-off lands but in this kingdom united by fear, fires blazed. The forgotten queen remained in chains, and singing and music were no more. It is said she is there to this day.

Introduction

As a matter of principle, I cannot continue to work with the Anglican church.[1]

These extraordinary words were from Mr Gus John, a respected author and academic. They formed part of a powerful counter-attack by Gus John targeting the current ABC Justin Welby as reported in the *Guardian* on 3 December 2019. Comments made by the archbishop over social media activated a reaction in John, who for many years had been a key consultant and supporter of the church's Committee for Minority Ethnic Anglican Concerns, known as CMEAC.

John wrote to Elizabeth Henry, the Church of England's national advisor on minority ethnic issues, saying he could no longer serve as a lay member of the church's Committee for Minority Ethnic Anglican Concerns. He stated that the church's record on combating racism was 'no less woeful now than it was 30 years ago'. 'Black and global majority people in the church, whether as clergy, laity or employees, are still experiencing discrimination and exclusion, benign and sugar-coated or otherwise, at every level of organisation in the church and yet, their active presence in communion with the church is responsible for its survival and buoyancy in many communities.'

This volley of devastating combination punches may stun, but will not floor, the white Church of England hierarchy. The English establishment will rally to discredit and distance itself from Gus John and his supporters. Black and brown clergy will cheer, or wince, or draw their curtains, apply the bolts on the door, and lock themselves away in fear, wondering if John's detonation will cause them to become collateral damage. A good friend and mentor once told me, 'You don't pull the tail of a lion' – meaning do not challenge the system as it will rear up and demolish you. But what if there is another lion and the tail you are pulling is Aslan's tail? What if there is a higher power than even the highest powers in the land? What if there is not only a distant family tree to draw on, but a family sea of supporters to swim within? The elite English establishment can feel all-consuming in its attempts at martial, cultural, economic and religious dominance to the appropriation or eradication of other forms of life and expression.

In this book I will be looking backwards over the 30-year period referenced by Gus John. I will be looking around at people of colour, and looking forward to what a new type of Church for all, and with all, and by all could be, within communities in which we live, the colleges where clergy train, and the churches that people like myself lead.

It is the night ...
White superiority
British aristocracy
Take aim,
Blame BAME,
You're colour blind?
Your colour binds!
When black is lack,
Stretched on the rack,
Seen through your eyes,
Black lives are lies,
Fluency in your language
doesn't mean it's our mother tongue,
The system is unequal, bring the sequel,
are you brave enough to get the job done?

BraveSlave[2]

* * *

I remember attending the church youth group bonfire night trip as a teenager. I was there with two older cousins, toffee apple in one hand and sparkler in the other. As our sparklers died, we retreated a little way from the fire. We were cold and huddled together, equipped with hats, scarves and gloves. The evening wore on and it was time to board the minibus to return to church. The white youth leader shouted out our names, as he couldn't find us. We were mere feet away from him. We stepped forward into the light of the fire and he laughingly said: 'Because you're black and it's dark, you lot are invisible, unless you keep smiling.' We all laughed and boarded the bus – this was a very familiar comment to me: 'Unless you smile, we cannot see you.'

There are many black church members hidden in the shadows of their congregations awaiting someone who knows them by name to call them into visibility, and invite them into a sense of calling and vocation. I have been smiling for a very long time, seeking to remain visible, loved and liked. My face is aching, and the smiles are turning into tears.

The Church of England is being encouraged to take inclusion seriously. In the last year, at a church I led in Suburbia, we had a visit from head office to our church council meeting. These visits can feel a little like an inspection. We had documents stacked high on tables, inventories, open registers, and details of works done on and in the building, which we refer to as the fabric. I am the only person of a visible minority back-ground within the group. The senior figure asked the group: 'How are we doing on diversity in this church?' A colleague of mine, without skipping a beat, pointed at me and responded: 'He answers that!' Everyone laughed, and I was plunged into darkness, smiling for grim life. I too laughed, my laugh a little louder than the others, attempting to mask the discomfort the playful riposte had prompted. Something of my organic fabric felt torn at that moment; the diversion caused by the laughter meant we did not think about the question, now buried beneath the mirth. We clambered back onto more settled questions and responses, questions we had answered before, variations on established themes. The question remains unanswered. I am not the answer, and I dare propose a better question:

3

'How are we doing on equality in this church?'

By 'this church' I mean the white historic church. Diversity can assume the need for a simple horizontal relationship to be created, whereas equality questions the vertical dimensions of the engagement. Who of the pair meeting, or the people group represented, has society imbued with the higher status in any given transaction? Who has society demoted and muted? This is not simply black and white, this is internalised.

I went to the Island of Nevis in the West Indies as a placement during my training for ministry. I was sponsored by a mission agency, then called the United Society, formerly the United Society for the Propagation of the Gospel, or USPG for short. This is an old mission agency that began as SPG and had a charter that prized white lives over black during the transatlantic slave trade. It was top-down mission, it was hierarchical, and blacks were very much at the bottom. It was compromised by short-term political power and economic concerns that made it complicit in the slave trade.[3] They have since travelled a long way in their thinking and undergirding philosophy. However, some of the white superiority of their founding fathers still awaits exorcism and laying to rest. I travelled to Nevis with a white man, also sponsored by the same mission agency, who was on the adjacent Island of St Kitts for the same month's duration. Towards the end of the month he and I met up to compare notes. We had had very different experiences. He shared the good treatment he had received everywhere. He had found it difficult to get to know what was going on because wherever he went he became the centre of attention; the programme he went to observe would immediately be tailored around him. He went to schools and was applauded and looked up to; he went to churches and found ready and receptive congregations. His presence alone would command respect and the black congregations expected to learn from him. When it was my turn to share, I offered how many people that I met were incredulous of my calling and suspicious of my credentials. The short dreads I sported caused some cultural dissonance. On a couple of occasions, I was laughed at when I spoke about my journey towards ordination. So there among my 'own' people it was harder for them to accept my ministry as on an equal footing to that of my white colleague. He and I were living out the centuries-old roles of master and slave. He was cocooned and celebrated, I was a puzzle and denigrated.

James Baldwin expresses the process of objectification I felt and the coronation my friend experienced as:

> I thought of white men arriving for the first time in an African village, strangers there as I am a stranger here, and tried to imagine the astounded populace touching their hair and marvelling at the colour of their skin. But there is a great difference between being the first white man to be seen by Africans and being the first black man to be seen by whites. The white man takes the astonishment as tribute, for he arrives to conquer and to convert the natives, whose inferiority in relation to himself is not even to be questioned, whereas I, without a thought of conquest, find myself among a people whose culture controls me, has even, in a sense, created me, people who have cost me more in anguish and rage than they will ever know, who yet do not even know of my existence.[4]

There are allusions to a slave past here – the old scripts one has to actively work against to be truly liberated. The slave owner acted as God to the slave. A white slave-master's words are recorded:

> Even after slavery had been abolished ... did I not tell him? What business has he to think, or to judge, or to set up his conscience after I have commanded him! The slaveowner demands obedience of body and soul ...[5]

Emotional labour

Emotional labour is the suppression of feelings between worker and customer or client. It is the neutral or friendly mask one wears in spite of the discomfort, displeasure, or even distress one may feel during an interaction. It is the deployment of mental resources to keep smiling when one is internally suffering. Those of us in relationships may be able to appreciate this troupe in the domestic sphere. In a helpful essay on emotional labour and race,[6] the authors consider an in-depth study of the world of aviation and the institution of law. They describe the regular micro-racisms that people face, like a spoken distrust of a black pilot's competence, for instance, or a comment about where a person is from, or when are they going back home. These mini assaults on one's personhood are death by a thousand paper cuts. The organisations have a supposed neutral liberalism, or an on-paper positive view of race and equality, but the felt experience and emotional burden on those black and minority ethnic members is significant. Part of the inbuilt worldview of these organisations is that black people are often angry and therefore irrational. When I described to a white theologian friend the idea of my book, his first response was 'Don't be angry.' I told him that anger is an emotion that is sanctioned. To his credit, he replied 'In that case, be *really* angry then.' The subjects of these emotional labour studies, time and time again, said they regularly chose to let offhand comments go, for fear of being labelled passionate or angry. The deeper fear is that resistance to the felt oppressive structure would leave them alienated or excluded. I asked a number of people of colour, mainly Church of England clergy, the following question:

Can you recall a painful comment or conversation with a white Christian peer about race and ethnicity?

Too many to name. But one that stayed with me was when I was an ordinand and was asked by the spouse of a tutor whether I'd started training for ministry in order to settle my residence status. Too many unchecked assumptions to even imagine where to start.

At theological college we had a visit from an incumbent of colour describing his context of urban ministry in London.

After the session a few ordinands were discussing how challenging aspects of his ministry appeared to be. One person said, 'I don't see why the college has called him here and we are forced to listen to him, it's irrelevant because where I will be doing ministry there are no such problems as we don't have any black people.'

I can recall many. Just a couple weeks ago I met an elderly white woman, shook her hand, and we exchanged names. She enthusiastically replied that she already knew which church I was based in. 'Really?' I said. 'How so?' 'Yes,' she said, I heard they had a black curate!' This of course not only bothered me (I really don't need to be constantly reminded that I am black), and reinforced whiteness as normative in the Church of England, but was also evidence that when white people speak about me, my skin colour is a primary topic of conversation. 'Did they tell you anything else about me?' I replied. She had no answer.

Yes, many. As a curate I was laughed at by the staff team for attending a BAME event and they could not understand why there was a need for such events or networks. Also as a curate, I was accused by a colleague of being our previous vicar's token BAME, and it was implied this was the only reason I was put forward for ordination.

I witnessed a white man, a parishioner in the church, wipe his hands (secretly) after shaking the hand of a black clergy member, as he was leaving the church.

At BAP [the three-day residential assessment for prospective clergy], I was asked why I didn't consider working in software or tech as 'your sort are good at it'. Talking about a vacancy: 'They had issues about an African priest but you're okay, no one would think you were an ethnic minority ...'

I do remember a white American Christian using expletives to say something about Tu Pac and other hip hop artists and how they were a negative influence on 'our' youth. This was painful as it was in a group discussion and it felt like this man had completely neglected to acknowledge the very recent ugly American history that had given birth and rise to artist such as Tu Pac.

The way in which it predominantly features is this: my white colleagues do not generally think further than their own experience, so do not see my needs. My experience is one in which I have to fight for the space to even express what I need, whereas most of the spaces provided are geared towards helping people with the 'known' issues. This simultaneously others and compounds the issues that the space should address for a person of colour.

These and many more scenarios are examples of the type that need the emotional labour shield to be at least 80 per cent charged to protect you from the whiteness wolves parading in sheep's clothing. They appear neutral, pastoral, cuddly even, but they sap one's strength and vitality. It is a whiteness that is at work in every arena of the Church of England, from its ruling council General Synod, to its theological colleges, and the way the Church of England operates in its communities. All privilege white concerns as the norm. Unless the status attributed to being white is examined, the white historic Church will continue to both consciously and unconsciously limit the voice, action and influence of her own non-white members, her women, her members of the queer community, her neuro-diverse, and those who live with disabilities. Critical whiteness studies are a tool to prise open the sealed can of white male dominance expressed in Synod, theological colleges and churches. What is the way to distil what is of value in English cultures, tip the rest away, and add it into a larger pot containing: contextual, postcolonial, global and liberation ingredients? The apparitions of a British imperial yesteryear are so powerfully resonant that one can be triggered into shock in an instant when one least expects it.

The time machine at St Paul's Cathedral

On Sunday 4 October 2015 I was invited, as part of the St Paul's Cathedral Black History Month, to be the preacher at Evensong. This being my first time preaching in such a grand setting, I went in a few days earlier in civvies and was slightly intimidated by the marching of the vergers and their team criss-crossing about their tasks with efficiency and speed. I plucked up courage to stand in the way of one such juggernaut, who I was delighted to discover was flesh and blood, and willing to accommodate my request. I wanted to stand in the pulpit and get a feel for such a platform and try a few of the evolving lines from my sermon. They removed the red cord barrier and escorted me up the staircase. They showed me the button for the microphone, where I could leave my sermon, where my glass of water could go, and so on, and then they left me, marched back down the steps and reapplied the barrier. Luckily, I rarely get vertigo – I was pretty high off the ground and felt a mile away from the congregation. As I familiarized myself, I happened to look up to the roof or canopy above the pulpit. My sense of intimidation grew and my sense of self shrank with what I read above me. There was a beautiful inscription which said:

For God and for Empire.

For some, that would no doubt be a source of pride, a high honour. To me it was code for supremacy and shame; a reminder of my slave ancestors being brutalised and traumatised by the buccaneering adventure-seekers who deposited enslaved Africans in the Caribbean to make sugar in order to satisfy the European sweet tooth, among other motives. I took a sharp intake of breath, then felt suddenly destabilised. I was caught in a type of tractor beam, pulling me back into an unfinished past. I long for the day when the empire's ongoing effects no longer advantage one group while disenfranchising others.

To love oneself as a black person in the UK is an act of resistance to the pressures and powers that are actively bearing down to disassemble whatever sense of identity one can muster. I have love for the black West Indian culture into which I was born and bred. This was expressed in Chapeltown, in Leeds, West Yorkshire, with aunts and uncles aplenty, of all shapes and sizes, and countless cousins. I did not grow up using the phrasing 'first, second, third cousin, once or twice removed', which individualises. No, I learned that you picked a relevant ancestor and linked as many people as you could to them. Other cultures may have an equivalent practice. I would be with a relative in the area and meet a stranger, and a sophisticated linking ritual would occur. 'Oh she's your cousin!' they would say. 'Oh she is to call Henry's sister's, aunty's father's uncle,' I struggled to keep up with the long list of apparent random linkages going back through the generations, until the common ancestor was located and therefore she and I were now cousins. And that was it. Less of a family tree, and more of a family sea. We were all in it together.

We traipsed from house to house, enjoying mountains of food, sometimes in dark valleys of despair, lit up with laughter and patois. We were constrained/disciplined by conservative forms of Christian religion. There was a longing, too, among the first-generation elders. A longing for back-home, the Islands, the sun, sea, surf and sarsaparilla. There were second-generation black-positive activists, based in places like the Mandela Centre, seeking to teach black history and black pride. I had no idea Mandela was even a person. I was within a Christian tradition which didn't watch the news, unless it involved Israel, Russia, or new technology, which all added up to Armageddon. The younger generation used words of affirmation to one another, our urban dictionary contained terms like 'Safe', which we would say as we fist-bumped, or 'Respect', or 'Easy'. On reflection we felt far from 'safe', there was not much which was 'easy' and on the whole we did not feel 'respect' from the wider society that we encountered. So we were establishing safety, respect and ease in our microclimate as much as we were able.

Today's youth, so I am told, use the word 'sick' a lot.

The Chapeltown community centre would put on holiday clubs – called 'play schemes' – for when school was out for the summer. We children would be excited to meet up with friends and go on the organised day trips, and we got to watch films on the coach. These were the days before regulation, and apparently youth and children's worker training, because for some reason the adults our parents trusted us with thought us kids would appreciate R rated movies. The coach had a fat TV monitor with VHS video built in, situated above and behind the driver's seat. The film we watched, and were spellbound by, was *Trading Places*. *Trading Places*, for the uninitiated, is about two men – a homeless black man, Billy Ray Valentine, played by Eddie Murphy, and a rich white man, Louis Winthorpe, who is played by Dan Ackroyd. It is about two worlds: the world of the underclass, the black male street hustlers and the white women street-workers, street violence; and the world of the upper middle classes, a white world, refined and elite. A place where crimes happened through paper and policy, suite violence.[7] The set-up was based around a bet between two old white brothers, Randolph and Mortimer Duke. They were playing God, like the Wizard of Oz before Toto pulled back the curtain revealing him to be impotent. They owned a large business and controlled the lives of all they surveyed. They disagreed on whether nature or nurture played the biggest role in shaping character, so they engineered a social experiment and made a dollar wager. Unbeknown to the men chosen as their pawns, the Duke brothers decided to temporarily reverse the fortunes of these two men.

They would take away the privilege and the prestige that came through access to the best that white society had to offer its members. They planned that, for a time, the young, ambitious and arrogant Louis Winthorpe would slum it; it would teach him some manners, then they would reinstate him.

This demonstrates that they had already decided that it was nature; Louis deserved the place and Billy Ray would never be fit. Unconsciously, in making it temporary, some part of them knew the black man would never be fit to truly lead. Even if, as happens, he proves he deserves to be there, they have already set his fate and determined his destiny, even if it goes against their best interests. They do not really want to make more cash, they want to make more clones.

The Church of England claims it wants to reverse the decline, build communities across its parishes and build congregations of purpose. However, those in power (and this is what I mean by variously using the term white, establishment, ruling classes, English elite) are not willing to Trade Places with those frozen out by the strong security measures that only grant access to a particular type of person. The Church of England does not want strong communities or empowered congregations, it wants clones. It cannot have both. What will happen when the rich white man leaves his castle, and the poor black man opens the gate to find staff arriving to call him Sir? Poor Louis loses privilege quickly. He winds up in jail, though innocent, and the only person who'd take him in is a white prostitute, Ophelia (played by Jamie Lee Curtis). His money is cut off, his private memberships are revoked, and he has to learn to hustle and resist the system that has made him, and now broken him. Billy Ray Valentine is inserted into the life Louis has been ejected from; he now works at the firm and has to navigate a very different world. He begins to excel, using instinct and a deep intelligence that propels him forward. He moves up the class ladder but does not lose his class, or his hustle. He does not know this is only an experiment. It is only a trial exercise, because we all know people are meant to stay where they are predestined to be – don't we?

Among the many ideas we have about God, there is a dominant strain undergirding a vision of this kind. One example of it flows from the pen of the white French scholar, theologian, and statesman from the sixteenth century, John Calvin. He held that a person's place in society was God-granted, rather than a function of human effort, advancement, or gift. Calvin said that we should

> honour men who have more than themselves because God has freely bestowed these special gifts of honour upon the elect. Thus the poor must yield to the rich; the common folk, to the nobles; the servants, to their masters; the unlearned, to the educated.[8]

This was a handy theory, since John Calvin himself was at the apex of the 'magisterium' of his day. He brought a sombre systemisation to Martin Luther's lively protestant revolution. Arts were out and executions were in, once he held the reins of power. If you have power and want to hold onto it, it is useful if your beliefs and lived convictions about God and theology match your place in the given society.

Back to mini-me, swinging his legs, littering the coach with popcorn bits watching this film *Trading Places*. The two men in the experiment go through a range of trials and eventually meet for the first time as peers. Equality is good, but equity is better, adjusting the conditions so everyone has a fair shot. When they meet as humans, one has lost his privilege and is now renouncing its trappings and embracing a broader view of who and what matters. And the Billy Ray who never lost his pride even in suppressed conditions demonstrates a wisdom parallel to, and in some ways superior to, the tried and tested normative business intelligence. He brings different eyes to the business social order and gives the company an advantage. The combination of Billy Ray Valentine's original thinking, with the opportunity to make a proper living, catalyses his sense of what is possible.

If the Church of England learns how to work effectively with its people of colour, the release of life and vitality that will flood through the church into the waiting world will be incredible. *Would* be incredible because, as Gus John says, for over 30 years the Church of England has had the Dukes' brothers approach: 'Let's give some of our people of colour a taste of white privilege, if they do well, great, it's probably our nurture of them that has led to their success. If they fail, fine, it's their nature that has caused them to fail.' In an interview, the Indian Episcopalian priest and justice advocate Winnie Varghese said:

> So, Kelly Brown Douglas, who I am so pleased to say is a friend, someone who I really, really admire, says it this way: you can't be white and be a Christian, it gets everyone's back up, it's a great technique and it's true. What she says is, whiteness is not a description of skin colour, you know,

whiteness doesn't have a category, it's not a thing, it's not an ethnic identity, it's not a language, or food. Whiteness is a tool of racism, whiteness is a tool of white supremacy, all kinds of whiteness are possible. You know, in the United States, Germans weren't white when they first came, they're white now. Italians weren't white when they came and have been made white. The Irish were not white when they first arrived. So, whiteness is a really flexible category. So flexible that my birth certificate, I'm sitting here next to you, about the same skin tone as you, my birth certificate says I'm white, I was born in Dallas, Texas but I'm not black or Mexican, which were the other categories. So a white woman very honestly wrote 'white' on my birth certificate. Whiteness is a claim to power, it's a claim to rightness, it's a racialised claim and there is no such thing as being white and being a Christian, you have to resist that identity.

When that identity is resisted, these two humans meet to work together effectively to create inclusive, generative, messy and magnificent community, and they also challenge and work to expose and demand changes from the complacent, colluding white hierarchy. What happens when those who have the privileges and power lose it, relinquish it, have it taken away? In the church, one example is Revd John Collins (1905–82). He grew up as a darling of the establishment, within a strong Tory family, and had ambitions of being Archbishop of Canterbury. He was chaplain to his Cambridge college, and by 26 was priest-in-ordinary to the king. His favourite hymn was 'All Things Bright and Beautiful'.

> The rich man in his castle,
> The poor man at his gate,
> God made them high and lowly,
> And ordered their estate.[9]

But he became friends with a radical Catholic priest who had been excommunicated, who challenged Collins' understanding of how society was ordered and how it could be reordered.

His socialist convictions outgrew his box and became a bridge to a new world and new version of himself. He started Christian Action, an organisation to support Christians engaging politically and socially, including protest and campaigning. He was in the bosom of the establishment and friends with Clement Attlee, who also being socialist pushed for John to become Canon John at St Paul's Cathedral, believing the bastion of Anglicanism could provide a platform for a new type of Christian Action to flourish. Collins was also one of the founders of CND along with Bertrand Russell and others.[10] Collins enjoyed the ongoing support of the establishment for his work. However, in 1950 Christian Action began to pursue race relations arising from the South African struggle.

The then Archbishop of Canterbury, Geoffrey Fisher, had been persuaded that black South Africans should find their own solutions inside South Africa and the outside church should not be involved as it might antagonise the Afrikaans government, making it harder for black Christians and churches to operate freely. That modus operandi is still in place today – leave the black community to solve their own problems without challenging the wider context which perpetrates or exacerbates those problems. So Archbishop Fisher decided protest and public denunciation of apartheid was out. However, John Collins disagreed and used the St Paul's platform for speakers from South Africa.[11] Collins himself preached a sermon directly criticising apartheid, and he attacked South Africa's prime minister Dr Malan. The papers nearly ran out of ink commenting on the sermon, and it contributed to investigations as to the extent to which Britain and South Africa were in partnership.[12] Nelson Mandela and others were risking prison by going into white only areas. The problem was that when these men were arrested, their families lost a breadwinner. Collins set up a fund to support the families of the boundary-crossing protesters.[13] But Collins had crossed a boundary himself, and the Church of England and those in the House of Lords were not amused by his identification with lawbreakers. Collins had a rule that civil disobedience was legitimate under repressive regimes but shunned the methods in a democratic society. Whatever his personal convictions, he was labelled as a troublemaker and had, in effect, traded places. In a collection of essays on his life we are told:

> Lord Halifax politely resigned from Christian Action, the Archbishops of Canterbury and Westminster withdrew their representatives: the movement and its creator were no longer respectable. The dream of storming and redeeming the establishment from within had dissolved.
>
> John was quite unrepentant, and soon a visit to South Africa convinced him even more deeply of the evils of apartheid and the duty of Christian resistance to it.[14]

While he was there he received the same treatment that black people in the UK were receiving. There were posters around Durban which said:

Collins, Go Home!

I long for more people like John Collins, people who move from a restrictive conservatism to a justice-based identification with those the church believes should solve their own problems, for their own good. Collins listened to the voices of the oppressed and allowed their needs to lead his response. He did not presume to come to this table trusting in his own righteousness. He lost his top spot as a future archbishop. He was strongly influenced by the white future Bishop of Stepney, Trevor Huddleston, who was influenced by a group of radical priests and missionaries. Collins did not gain the world on offer, but he did not lose his soul, his soul was knitted with his black South African brothers and sisters. Later he would discover his common cause with the American civil rights struggle. And just as he funded black and brown people to occupy white-only spaces, he added his support to Wilfred Wood, who would go on to become Britain's first black bishop.

I am now a black minister in the white Church of England, I have been since 2010. A family tree approach to life from a white worldview placed me out on a branch far from the trunk. Unlike the greetings slang I used in my youth, a number of my clergy colleagues of colour and I do not feel 'safe', 'respected', and it is definitely not 'easy'. It is more like we are 'sick'. Sick and tired of sitting on the coach as passengers, kept quiet as passive observers, munching popcorn as if we are children, while we are driven to God knows where, by God knows who. I and others have been watching this movie on repeat, and our cries of 'Are we nearly there yet?' fall on deaf ears.

Now I know we people of colour-definition are not the only group who have been knocking on the door of the church, burrowing under the walls, clambering over the fences, abseiling from the roof just to get in and say 'Here we are – present and correct.' As well as the BAME coalition, there is the LGBTIQ+ coalition, there is a coalition of women who have breached the walls; but there remain adults with a range of disabilities, and those from working-class communities, as well as the neuro-diverse, who are all seeking to break into fortress Church of England. Children and young people do not feel particularly represented either. It gets especially complicated when you have overlapping identities, you have to go to all the meetings and all the rallies, and suffer all of the disappointments!

And then you meet colleagues who are white, where white means power and a belief that they know what is best for all concerned when they should be there to listen and support. However, you can feel as if you are banging your head against a brick wall. This is a conversation I had with a senior leader with significant responsibility for the running of a multicultural diocese (a diocese is one of the 42 ancient regions that are captained by a bishop).

Me	What happens in your diocese in regards to inclusion and diversity?
Mr Avoidant	What do you mean?
Me	How are your staff and team who are black and minority ethnic supported?
Mr Avoidant	What do you mean?
Me	Well, in the civil service they work hard to offer support to those of different backgrounds.

Mr Avoidant   Yes, well, in the civil service it's a priority, for us it's important ... and what's more we think about all kinds of diversity so ethnicity sits alongside disability and gender.

Me   Oh, but I think ethnicity has its own particular hurdles to overcome.

Mr Avoidant   Well if you say that, whose diversity do you prioritise ... the British-born black person, the West African or the East African? There are so many cultural differences between them that you can't possibly cater to them all ...

Me   What if we spun it round to think about who fits most neatly into the roles, so what if the focus was white heterosexual men, and them understanding if they had any additional advantage?

Mr Avoidant   What do you mean?

Me   The *Guardian* brought out a report which said in many universities BAME students and lecturers suffered in silence feeling they are not afforded the same credit and respect as their white peers.

Mr Avoidant   What do you mean?

Me   The government launched a Race Disparity Audit [Mr Avoidant looks blank], you can Google it, it will give you clear statistical analysis of what those of black heritage need [Mr Avoidant continues to look blank].

At this point a white woman who was a mutual friend chimed in:

Ms Helpful White Interpreter   How about you consider the recruitment practices and ease the access for people of BAME backgrounds?

Mr NowHeGetsIt   Oh, I see, yes we could do something like that.

Mr Avoidant went on to describe a mission trip to the West Indian Island of Haiti and the sadness of the corruption there, seemingly without a thought for its history or the crippling tariff it paid to France for so long. As well as working with a charity that worked in Africa, he had also lived in a multicultural area for a time, though he felt like a fish out of water. It felt as if he was parading his credentials. However, the conversation we were having felt exhausting. I was having to constantly prove my point and perspective. His attitude to me felt very lopsided. I felt he was attempting to exert power over me that he seemed oblivious to within this conversation, and the contexts he had visited and was resident within.

As in *Trading Places*, if you are a clergy person of colour in the Church of England, some bishop has welcomed you aboard. Statistically speaking they are almost overwhelmingly likely to be white and male. If they are a good bishop, they will look to you to be an ally and perhaps a confidant, as they welcome your help to dismantle something with which they have become disillusioned. That has happened to me on a few occasions. It can be wearying being expected to do someone else's work for them, but perhaps it is better than other bishops who see no need for change and allow the system to run unchallenged or unquestioned for the benefit of themselves and their hoped-for future clones who will provide for them. Sometimes I wonder what it is we are we all trying to break into? And why? Should we follow Gus John and leave? And for white clergy who, like John Collins, are idealistic: have you assessed your ambition? Are you happy to remain in a church where the status quo is of a God who only whispers when injustice is felt and experienced? A lion with a lisp: is that the God you want to worship, honour, and obey? Are we acting in a sane way knowing we are within an institution which, post the murder of Stephen Lawrence, launched its own enquiry into its own institutional racism? The report by a Church of England committee entitled 'Called to Act Justly' has a number of descriptions of institutional racism. I have chosen the following ones:

Institutional racism could arise from overt acts of discrimination and/or hostility by individuals acting out their personal prejudices and from inflexible, 'traditional' ways of doing things, especially in tight-knit or long-standing communities.

Racism was sometimes fuelled by a mistaken 'colour blind' approach where everybody is treated the same instead of recognising and responding to individual needs.

Racism could be imbedded in laws, customs and practices in the structures, policies and processes, resulting in allegations of institutional racism regardless of the intentions of individuals.

Unwitting racism could arise from a lack of understanding, ignorance or mistaken beliefs; from well-intentioned but patronising words or actions; from a lack of familiarity with the behaviour or cultural traditions of people or families from Black or minority ethnic communities; and from unconscious racist stereotyping.

The report also holds the following statement:

And thus that The Archbishops Council has recognised that the Church of England, like other institutions in society, must accept the challenge of institutional racism and repent (GS Misc 625, 2000:2) ... regardless of the original intention of the personnel involved, there is little doubt that their policies or sometimes lack of policies nevertheless have damaging social consequences for the less powerful ethnic and racial minorities. It is ultimately on this level of policy that the church needs to reflect on its own theology, and thus its own praxis, if it is going to effectively deal with the institutional racism within its own structures.[15]

I am telling my version of the story of people of colour – some of whom I know and some know me. I am glad to be a member of a clergy of colour family sea, with Ugandans like John Sentamu, African Americans like Michael Curry, West Indians like Rose Hudson-Wilkin and Eve Pitts, Indians based in America like Winnie Varghese, or based here in the UK like Mukti Barton and many others. All brave souls who have and continue to shape my thinking and action and have helped keep me afloat when I was drowning. As for the black story, it feels like one way one could possibly ascend the ranks of the Church of England is to convert to whiteness. Until our institutions are reordered, our education systems, our political systems, and our church systems, a person of colour does not have the societal backing and reinforcement to flourish. John Collins lost something in terms of progression and reputation but he still had access to the social capital of the old boys' network. He still had access to white society, its institutions and its benefits. In fact, he attempted to bring black and brown people up to where he was, by opening his platform and sharing his privilege. There was no height so great that a big, strong, bold guardian angel would not intervene should he fall, and ensure he didn't strike his foot against a stone. On the other hand, there is not very much of the network effect for people of colour in the Anglican Church. There are a few recent examples, but there is a long way to go to provide the sense of insulation needed to take the necessary risks. If you want support as a clergy person of colour, you have little recourse other than to fit into the white structures of support that do not understand your wider needs. There has been an erosion of supportive groups within the Church of England.

Joseph Washington demonstrates that the Dukes' ideology, the idea that whites are better than blacks, stretches back quite a long way. He documents the following gravestone from 1780 which says:

In memory of
Caesar
Here lies the best of slaves
Now turning into dust
Caesar the Ethiopian craves
A place among the just.
His faithful soul has fled
To realms of heavenly light

And by the blood that Jesus shed
Is changed from Black to White.[16]

The Church of England can operate as a Club, and equates whiteness with power. The hierarchy is so steep, and at the pinnacle only the sovereign is precariously balanced, supported by the English establishment just beneath, with our generals, judges, vice-chancellors, our bishops, our parliamentarians, our heads of business, newspaper editors and publishers. Where do the rest of us go? Is it time to invert the triangle? Is it time to join with Mary in her Magnificat – her manifesto where she describes bringing the powerful down from their places? What if the aforementioned groups, often white English men of a narrow trajectory, flattened their mountain, so that the mountain of the Lord could be more clearly seen? The mountain where Aslan is roaring in pain, bound on the stone table, as whiteness binds him, and binds all who seek to follow him in the way of the cross, rather than the way of the crown.

As you travel through this book, you will encounter history, biography, theology, some chapters mystical, some fictional, some polemical, and some hopefully comical, to convey an insider's view of being in the hold, and sometimes on the deck, of the Ghost Ship.

Ghost Ship

In this chapter we learn why the book is titled as it is. We learn of a little-known avoidable tragedy at sea and how it becomes a guiding myth for much of our discussion.

Remember, Remember

In this chapter we consider the transatlantic slave trade and the UK's part in it, and ask the question why society seeks to blank it out. There is also an introduction to Eve Pitts, whose mystical encounter has led to nothing short of a movement of honouring those who have gone before us.

No Pain Allowed

I recount an incident where I was challenged by a senior Church of England leader to tone down my protest. I explore what it means to become empty of one's identity.

Slave Ship

We consider something of the journey to ordination. We look at the identity that is jettisoned to join the (Club).

Intermission: A Conversation with Rose Hudson-Wilkin

I have an engaging talk with the Bishop of Dover.

Get Out of My House!

In this chapter we remember the history of 30 years ago and the battle mounted by the people of colour associated with the General Synod.

Reimagining Reimagining Britain

Here we examine among other things a book by Justin Welby called *Reimagining Britain*, to understand something of his current thinking with regards to inclusion and community.

You Cannot Judge a Book by its Cover

We will be introduced to two people who on the surface you may not think hold the views they do. We learn about how their experiences have formed their identities and attitudes.

Buried Alive

This chapter considers the lure of the shiny churches in the Church of England. How they are a death trap for black and brown clergy, and what we can do to overcome the white saviour figures.

Token Gesture

In my family we love the saying: 'It ain't the size of the dog in the fight, it's the size of the fight in the dog.' However, are we just too small to make any real impact?

Conclusions?

Be aware that there are no answers which have not already been proposed. And there are no questions which have not already been posed.

Notes

1 John, G. (2020), 'Academic quits C of E body over chief rabbi's Labour antisemitism comments', *Guardian*. Available online at: www.theguardian.com/world/2019/dec/03/academic-quits-c-of-e-body-over-chief-rabbis-labour-antisemitism-comments.

2 An unpublished collection of poems.

3 www.uspg.org.uk/about/history/.

4 Baldwin, J. (1955), *Notes of a Native Son – Stranger in the Village*, Boston: Beacon Press, p. 21.

5 Erskine, N. (1998), *Decolonizing Theology*, Eritrea: Africa World Press, p. 57.

6 Evans, Louwanda and Leo Moore, Wendy (2015), 'Impossible Burdens: White Institutions, Emotional Labor, and Micro-Resistance', *Social Problems*, 62(3), pp. 439–54.

7 'State, Suite, and Street violence' is from various works by Johan Gultang, the peace studies thinker and practitioner.

8 Calvin, John (1536/1960), *Institutes of the Christian Religion*,

Vol. 20, ed. John T. McNeill, trans. Ford Lewis Battles, Philadelphia: Westminster Press, 3.7.1–5.

9 Cecil Frances Alexander, from 'All Things Bright and Beautiful' (1848).

10 Henderson, Ian (1976), *A Man of Christian Action, Canon John Collins – the man and his work*, Cambridge: Lutterworth Press, p. 102.

11 Henderson, *A Man*, p. 47.

12 Ibid.

13 Ibid.

14 Ibid., p. 108.

15 'Called to Act Justly: A challenge to include minority ethnic people in the life of the Church of England', report by the Stephen Lawrence Follow-Up Staff Group, April 2003, London: Church House Publishing, p. 6.

16 Washington, J. (1984), *Anti-Blackness in English Religion 1500–1800*, New York: The Edwin Mellen Press, p. 351.

I

Ghost Ship

They jostle on the upper deck,
Whilst below their shoes are wet,
The boat overfull, passengers and crew,
Sisters in Holy Orders scold children,
who take in the view,

They settle on the upper deck,
Whilst below their knees are wet,
The boat overfull, passengers and crew,
observe a shark fin, not one but two,

They tumble from the upper deck,
Whilst below their ears are wet
The boat emptying, its passengers and crew,
The waters claiming more than a few.

Their journeys unfinished,
Lost where they lie,
One hundred souls slumber,
The sea breeze mingles their cries.

BraveSlave

Martin Luther King in his private moments displayed a level of
doubt over his goals and aims. In a conversation he had with
singer Harry Belafonte, Belafonte reports King told him:

I've come upon something that disturbs me deeply. We have
fought hard and long for integration, as I believe we should

have, and I know we will win, but I have come to believe that we are integrating into a burning house ... Until we commit ourselves to ensuring that the underclass is given justice and opportunity, we will continue to perpetuate the anger and violence that tears the soul of this nation. I fear I am integrating my people into a burning house.

Belafonte added, 'That statement took me aback. It was the last thing I would have expected to hear, considering the nature of our struggle.'

Belafonte then asked King, 'What should we do?' And King replied that we should 'become the firemen. Let us not stand by and let the house burn.'[1]

I find this exchange fascinating because it begins with an acknowledgement of a problem but ends with a desire to play a part in fixing the problem for America (which I assume means white Americans with power). I am beginning to wonder if the better approach would have been not 'Let us not stand by and let the house burn' but 'Let's build a new house and urge those in the burning house to escape.' And was the problem really poverty, or was it a system that perpetuates poverty?

King could also have used the metaphor of a sinking ship. The 42 dioceses of the Church of England, which includes the Diocese in Europe, are at different levels of readiness for the task of creating a church that is represented by all and produced by all. There is a ghost ship. Of the vessels that the Church of England is inviting people of colour to join, many are not shipshape. They look good from the outside, but they are overcrowded, and the black and brown clergy are shoved below-deck as second- or third-class crew. The materials are inadequate. We need a new Ark. I am a descendant of enslaved black Africans, who travelled on ships from West African ports with free white Europeans from Scottish and French shores. Nevis is the Island where both of my parents were born and raised, then a part of the empire, now a member of the Commonwealth. Nevis is a member of a two-island federation that includes the adjacent Island of St Kitts. It also happens to be the smallest nation in the Western Hemisphere. There is a 12-mile stretch of water between the Islands' capitals, Basseterre and Charlestown. Both Islands have a collective population of around 50,000. Between the Islands, the waters are haunted.

Yes, I did say haunted.

The Islands are luxury holiday destinations for cruise ship travellers, honeymooners, the rich and the powerful; predominantly, though not exclusively, white westerners. The Islands' buildings and landscape bear the gruesome physical scars of the transatlantic people-for-profit trade. The Islands nurse a deep grief that can be difficult to detect beneath the smiles and warm welcomes. There is great pride in this place of natural and cultivated beauty.

There is a ghost ship in the water and the souls are not at rest. Growing up with my mother in Chapeltown in Leeds, I loved it when visitors from the Island of Nevis came to our home from back-home (an affectionate reference to the Island). This was in the 1980s when exotic fruits were less common and less known about in the UK; if you were a black person who could afford to regularly buy exotic fruit, you didn't live in Chapeltown. It was also an aviation wild west where, if you could fit the fruit in your suitcase or holdall, you could bring it with you. The X-ray scanners were simpler back then. We had a trick of wrapping contraband fruit in a thick towel and the X-ray scanners or operators were none the wiser. Before our guests arrived, my mother would have me grate ginger, mix it with a small bowl of Demerara brown cane sugar, then add it to water-filled containers. I would mix it all together again and then strain it into jugs loaded with ice, to make sweet ginger beer to be presented to the guests upon arrival.

Our guests would bring bulging bags full of fruit; exotic for us, normal for them. My favourite guests were the ones who brought mangoes from back home, with names I think particular to the Island: Jopane, Roundball, and Stringy mango, for instance. Another treat that came with the guests was that we would get to enter the hallowed front room. If you are of Caribbean heritage you'll know about this; if you have a Caribbean family member or friend, ask them about it. The front room was the holy of holies; whatever chaos or concerns filled the rest of the house, this was a shrine to all things West Indian. It was a protected habitat reserved for visitors and usually off-limits. West Indians cared for their front rooms like environmental activists care for the planet. The room was decked out in West Indian standard-issue furniture, flowery wallpaper, plastic flowers and plastic doilies. We had a radiogram fitted with a record player in the corner, often playing one of the following music artists: Jim Reeves, Jimmy Swaggart, Oral and Richard Roberts, Edwin Hawkins, Mighty Clouds of Joy, or the Sensational Nightingales (yes, these are real names of real artists).

Most often played were the two Jimmy's, Swaggart and Reeves, and Oral and his son Richard Roberts. They were white American men who were respected preachers within Mum's circles, who used to imitate black forms of oratory and tap into black poverty to exploit women like my mother. She was taken in by the music and persuaded into being a sponsor for their endeavours, believing that she was investing in the future health and wealth of herself and her son. We did have one Jesse Jackson 'Operation Push' record. Remember Jesse? A precursor to Obama, with a Tom Selleck moustache, he had too much bite and fight for the American electorate. On the album he preached and sang a message of black power and black beauty, but we didn't listen to that album much. We also had our crockery and glassware in glass display cabinets with gold effect framing. We were economically suppressed but house-proud. I often think of my black and minority ethnic clergy colleagues as like those items in the display cases – so much to offer, wanting to be used and enjoyed, but stuck behind glass and locked away.

My mother's qualifications, which she had worked hard for in her late teens back home, were rejected in the UK, although the tests she passed and the certification she had earned were designed and authorised by the UK. So she had to struggle to earn a living, and had to learn how to live anew in a strange land. We had long black velvet wall hangings with a picture of our home Island on them, a boat and a palm tree as standard.

We had a set of round trays with the young Charles and Diana on them after their wedding. And religious art, we loved the religious artwork, the characters were entirely white but we didn't care – we loved it all. We had the 3D-effect picture of Jesus in the garden of Gethsemane. We must have known that suffering was our lot too.

The front room was a preservation of hope and a lifeline to home. I think the plastic flowers were there because they were durable. We could not afford luxuries like fresh flowers, and besides, I had allergies. The front room was a connection to the wider world: the music, the long-wave radio, the conversations held there, the ginger wine drunk there, the food from back home seen in there but consumed in the kitchen or the back room for fear of mess and spillage.

It was a little embassy, with two monarchs: King Jesus and the queen. We had a gloriously outsized picture of Her Majesty wearing her crown and sitting with Prince Philip off to her side in military garb. We also had a huge picture of a beautiful blond, bronzed guardian angel: hyper-alert, watching over two cherubic-looking white English children, a girl with hair in bunches and her arm over a little blond boy wearing shorts with pulled-up socks (her brother, one assumes). They were ambling towards a broken bridge and hadn't noticed. The angel was primed to respond and spring to the rescue like one of today's helicopter parents who want to install CCTV in their child's nursery. You can't see them but you know they are there watching. I guess somewhere there is a picture of the black and brown kids at the other side of the bridge blundering forward towards oblivion, and the aforementioned angel nowhere to be seen.

The visitors would bring food and laughter. When they began to settle in, I would usually slink away, released from Mum's watchful gaze to get up to mischief or retreat into the latest Marvel comic, usually Spider-Man (another white hero), to avoid the 'big people' talk regarding politics and various personages. If I was unlucky, I would be called back to partake in the obligatory prayers, which would include holding sweaty palms. The prayers would be long, long improvised monologues. I was expected to show off my emerging orator-ical skills and elicit Amens from the guests to demonstrate how well Mum was doing at raising me as a Christian boy with manners. Mum would often lead unaccompanied songs and I would enjoy attempting to harmonise. She would then give them a goodie bag to take back with them. Ginger beer was a staple, along with oranges, perhaps a blue box of American-style macaroni cheese, and ham in a tin with a little key to turn as the gelatine oozed out.

Being an introvert – and having spent the last of my energy in the prayer time – I would internally flop when someone struck up another conversation as we stood in the hallway on the ridged, clear, carpet protector (yet another West Indian staple). There was a recurring topic that would come up – the MV *Christena*. She was a boat that had sunk – the greatest boat-ing disaster in the English-speaking Caribbean. On Saturday, 1 August 1970, in the afternoon, she was making her last trip of the day. The boat was already full, but there was a demand to cross on the last voyage and the ticket collectors were happy to continue collecting until the boat was dangerously over-crowded. She could safely hold 155 people; on that day there were over 320 people aboard. There was no blond guardian angel preventing those people boarding a broken boat, and it sank. Ninety-one people were rescued and survived, 57 dead bodies were recovered and named, 66 dead bodies were recov-ered but were unidentifiable – there were sharks in the water.

As for the hundred or so who remained, a report stated:

A number of bodies were trapped inside the sunken wreck-age, and these bodies were left in place. A decision was made to leave the boat and [the entrapped] bodies undisturbed.[2]

The waters are haunted by those aboard the ghost ship. August 2020 marks the 50th anniversary of this tragic disaster, which impacts Nevisians and Kittitians to this day. So many were lost that no family was left untouched either directly or as a part of the collective trauma.

I am aboard an old, grand ship built to explore new worlds.

A ship with two rulers. But who can serve two masters? My front room held two visions: a suffering human, sweating drops of blood in anguish, and a radiant sovereign, deity-like, commandeering our front room with her military husband in the wings (if memory serves, Prince Philip had a dress sword hanging from his belt). It could be argued that as the established church, the Church of England has merged the two rulers.

If the Church of England serves two masters, and has effectively merged the two, in a sense it operates with a kind of multiple personality disorder and has to war against the various instincts and passions that such a merger might lead to. Or perhaps it is worse than this, and it is more like the ginger beer I made, everything is all mixed up together and it has to be tipped out and remade.

There was another piece of art in my home, this time in the back room, and it contained the following quote:

Christ is the Head
of this house,
the unseen guest at every meal
the silent listener to every conversation.

My mum would point to this piece of terror art and use it as a motif of her and God's total surveillance. So whatever I was getting up to at home, I was being watched. Here is a purely *hypothetical* list: if I was creeping downstairs when she was asleep to watch a movie that my tender eyes should've been protected from (my summer play schemes had ruined that), Christ was spying on me. Or if as a teen I dared sneak into the house and dared to drink a beer (and I don't mean a ginger beer), while she was at her church Bible study, Christ was aghast and deeply, deeply sad. But because my mum and I had merged the monarchs, Christ was more the Prince Philip with the dress sword, subtly protecting the queen's right to all she surveyed, rather than the Jesus crying on his knees. What if we had subscribed to the suffering Jesus on his knees? Imagine how I might have heard the quote then?

What if the white elite were to privilege the leadership of

those who are suffering on the vessel? What if we asked: who are the 'unseen guests' in the Church of England? Do they sit at our tables, shuffle into our pews, attend our social events? Can we seek to make visible the invisible? Who are the 'silent listeners' to our conversations, in our committees, on our cricket pitches, in our private members' clubs, our church fêtes, in our school assemblies, or our synods, filling the kettles in our kitchens, cleaning our church halls, taking money from us in the coffee shops where we regularly have our meetings?

The church has a decision to make as to which path it will take. The path of power, privilege and prestige – the way of the Crown, which is the way of the predator. Or the path of pain, people and paying the price – the way of the Cross. This is the way of the prey, a chosen or imposed vulnerability. The Church of England is like the MV *Christena*. There are some who follow one path and feel safe aboard the upper deck, and then there are the rest of us who are getting wetter below deck. We people of colour who are clergy in the Church of England have been recruited, our photos were taken before we embarked, we waved, and once we were out of view of those on the shore, we were ushered downstairs below deck and into the dark. This boat, the Church of England, is not fit for purpose. It cannot accommodate the black and brown passengers it already has, yet it continues to beckon for more and we gleefully climb aboard, unaware of the fact that this boat is taking on water and many of us will not survive the trip. We will leave, we will suffer mentally, we will cower in corners. Our confidence will be destroyed, we will blaze with anger only for cool white western rationalism to drown us in cold, calculated, critique and censure.

I know that, because I have seen these patterns, I have heard these stories, I have lived this life.

A constant refrain coming from all quarters of the church is that it is in decline. This is usually expressed in falling numbers. As priests we have to submit our numbers to HQ, outlining how many are attending our services, and that number is going down, on the whole across the board. Can I offer another way to consider this?

It is not that the church is in decline, it is not only that the numbers are going down, it is the Church of England *itself* that is sinking. Even those shiny churches on the upper, upper deck with the better views and the built-in swimming pools, are in danger. The middle deck is the Church of England as is, and the lower down in the decks you go, the darker and the poorer the passenger becomes.

The church is sinking, but those in the bottom decks will drown first. Our bodies will haunt the waters of the Church of England. I am delighted SCM Press entrusted me to write on race. Is this a new conversation? There has been a lot written on this in recent years in British society at large; Anthony Reddie on Brexit, Reno Edo Lodge on Race, Ben Lindsey's response on Race and the UK church, David Isiorho, others like Nels Abbey, Afua Hirsch, and artists like Camille Barton, politicians, whether a David Lammy or a Shaun Bailey, and academic artists and activists like George the Poet, and Akala, or novelists like Malorie Blackman, to name a few. But this conversation goes right back, and writing by people like David Olusoga can demonstrate how far back. For SCM Press the earliest book I found on the topic is *Christianity and the Race Problem* by J. J. Oldham, published in 1924. Will I, or a contemporary, need to write another book in 2024? Is this inevitable? The suffering and pain experienced by many black and brown Anglicans today will be experienced by some white Anglicans tomorrow. Although with independent financial security, and a society of heroes and inspiration to draw from, and a backdrop which mirrors those white people, they won't die when the church goes down. They have access to life-jackets and lifeboats.

The MV *Christena* did not sink by accident, it was made with poor materials. If you were on the lower decks you always had wet feet. There were those who were concerned with the boat's safety, who petitioned Whitehall (the island was British, and we were British subjects). The letters sent were not taken seriously. Out of sight, out of mind. The commission to investigate the factors that led to the sinking included this in the official reporting. But there were also black people on site who were rewarded for selling tickets and ensuring as many as possible were on board.

So what does this mean? If the ship is damaged, if there are two approaches to ministry, which will endure, the cross or the crown? Should we continue to call for more black and brown leaders to join the ranks and be ushered into the lower decks? It is my firm conviction that the dioceses of the Church of England need to take stock of how seaworthy their vessels are for transporting black and brown clergy. Should some dioceses stop recruiting altogether until extensive work is done? Like the MV *Christena*, the call has gone out time and time again for radical root and branch changes to be made in order to truly have a vessel that provides adequate shelter in the storms and gets us all to our destinations in one piece.

How can black and brown Anglicans know that a diocesan vessel is safe to sail? What is the kite mark to give that assurance? July 2010 was the moment I was ordained into the Church of England. Ten years later, at the time of publication, this is not improving. In fact, in a number of ways it has got worse. There are more black and brown clergy joining the church. In the state the Church of England is in, black and brown clergy have to factor racial injustice into the deal. If you are black or brown and considering ordination in the Church of England, can I suggest you find out the facts, and go in with your eyes open. If you are already on board, make yourself safe – there is safety in numbers. Do not let this be your only source of identity. If you are charged with selling tickets for this trip, can I ask you to pull down the shutters, put up an 'out to lunch' sign, and ask hard questions of where the new recruits will end up.

Why am I looking back? Is there any benefit to considering what has gone before? An English idiom, 'let sleeping dogs lie', comes to mind. But what if the sleeping forms beneath the table are people? And the sleep is a form of hibernation, due to lack of sustenance. Those of African descent know the story of the dehumanising event of the transatlantic slave trade. It does not feel that far away. Like those of us who have lost a loved one, no matter the distance in time, the proximity in mind is what makes the slave trade more real. And it is to this event to that we now turn.

Notes

1 AUTODIDACT 17 (2020), *Dr Martin Luther King Jr: 'I fear I am integrating my people into a burning house'*, Amsterdamnews.com, available online at: http://amsterdamnews.com/news/2017/jan/12/ dr-martin-luther-king-jr-i-fear-i-am-integrating-m/.

2 Arthur Anslyn, Captain of the *Caribe Queen*, who was hired by the Commission of Inquiry to dive the site after 1 August. https:// en.m.wikipedia.org/wiki/Arthur_Anslyn. Browne, Whitman T. (2013), *The Christena Disaster*, iUniverse, Bloomington.

2

Remember, Remember

Antichrist

The monstrosity of transatlantic slavery is not securely dead and buried in the cemetery of world history. The coffin has been shattered. Its inhabitant refuses to die. The tomb is empty, heaps of disturbed earth mark the escape. It is an ever-spawning, undead entity, stalking and devouring the living. It is an antichrist whose regeneration leaves death in its wake. It no longer lives on through its creators – the merchants, philosophers, clergy, monarchy, scientists, judges, lecturers, and journalists in the thirteenth century – but does so now through their descendants. The contagions of transatlantic slavery infected institutions with anti-black racist ideologies to justify selling black humans for their own interests and profit. Transatlantic slavery is venomous. How many of us have been poisoned and find our humanity marred by its scratch or bite? We need an antidote, because the anti-human heart of the ongoing legacy of the genocidal transatlantic slavery beats on, and this sickness, unless addressed, will end in death.

Parishes can confine us and feel more like plantations, with an old master in the big house, an overseer, and the expectation of one's labour being of greater value than one's life. In the fifteenth century Pope Nicolas V bought some of the first slaves of the transatlantic slave trade for his friends. With this endorsement the slave trade was off to a flying start. Eventually England took the lead and became the biggest market for slavery. Most of its slaves were offshore in the Caribbean. Out of sight was out of mind for the British public. In America, while the North was safe to an extent, the South was not. The slaves had a solidarity with one another, and a hope of freedom through the underground railroad. The British slaves in the Caribbean had no such hope. The lucrative nature of the emerging enterprise was too much to pass up on.

The Church of England was the dominant ecclesial force during the transatlantic slave trade

Some Church of England clergy believed that the 'savage brutishness' of the slaves ruled out even conversion. On the other hand, the clergy often acquiesced with the powerful status quo of the slave system as silent onlookers.[1] The system bound white people in red tape just as the system bound the slaves in red welts. Bishops and abbots were restricted from emancipating slaves even if they wanted to. However, they could own slaves for ministry tasks.[2] Why was the church not free to object and protest this vile horror? Too often it was because the church was hand in glove with money. And 'he who pays the piper calls the tune'.

The Society for the Propagation of the Gospel

The mighty English empire had a problem. Englishmen found themselves scattered around the world without sufficient access to Anglicanism. The charter for SPG signed by King William IV noted that he had been:

> credibly informed, that in many of our Plantations, Colonies, and Factories beyond the Seas, the Provision for Ministers is very mean, and some of them are wholly destitute.[3]

There was a greater fear that Englishmen would be converted to Catholicism, and as always a new project needed investment. An afterthought was: what if some the slaves were converted? How would that affect their status? Might this hinder and disrupt the aspirations of the various parts and partners in the slave enterprise? So an Act of Parliament was sought that said:

for the more Effectual Conversion of the Negros and other servants, the Plantations; and particularly, that Slaves Baptized should nevertheless continue bound in Service to their respective Masters as before Baptism.[4]

The Lord Archbishop of Canterbury ensured that the Society at its inception could be funded by 'the eminent Merchants, especially such of them as traded into the Plantations'.[5]

We speak of the 'established church', but it was the relationship between church, state, monarchy, the wealthy capitalists and the judiciary which was more established. The apparent different parts of the puzzle were actually pieces of the same hallowed whole.[6] The fear, however, that converting slaves would be bad for business did not go away, so that in 1727 the Bishop of London pronounced:

> Christianity does not make the least alteration in Civil Property ... it continues persons just in the same State as it found them ... [it] is a freedom from the bondage of Sin and Satan ... but as to their outward condition ... whether bond or free ... becoming Christians makes no manner of change.[7]

In fact, to internalise and ensure the process, Washington gives an example of a Negro prayer.

> O Thou great God, the Maker and Lord of all creatures, I, a poor sinner, black in body, and still blacker in sin, would humbly try to worship thee ... and make the land of my slavery, the place of my true freedom ... Bless my master, and all that are his. Make me a faithful servant; and teach me to remember, that what good thing so ever any man doth; the same shall he receive of the Lord. Amen.[8]

If the line about freedom confuses you, Washington describes part of the catechism where the assessor asks: 'How can you be free and bound both?' The expected answer is: 'I am free indeed, although my body and services may be at the command of another.'[9]

The carol 'O Holy Night' has the line 'the slave is still our brother'. This is a jarring and distressing line ameliorated by the gentle 6/8 arpeggio undergirding it. I do not know many hymns which directly discuss the material fact of slavery. There are a number of hymns I know that discuss spiritual bondage, but how many songs can we list that mention physical and brutal slavery? I wonder if this is because this carol came from outside the church. Its author, Placide Cappeau, was a socialist and wine merchant. He had not been conditioned to look at things through the lens of the status quo, meaning that he lacked the blind spots of the insider, he didn't ignore white elephants or black slavery. He had not been conditioned to look where he was told to look. When the Catholic Church learned who the author was, they attempted to ban it. However, the attempted repression of the song only caused it to grow all the more popular. But for so many white Christians the slave is not their brother or sister. Many would say, 'Slavery is over, let us move on.'[10]

'When You Go Home, Tell Them Of Us And Say / For Your Tomorrow, We Gave Our Today'[11]

I was sitting in a train carriage ready for my journey to begin. As the train doors closed a shadow darted across my peripheral vision, one moment there was clear space, the next a tall gaunt, weathered figure was planted, swaying slightly as the train moved. I was surprised when from such a rough-looking man a polished silver voice emerged: He said:

> I am an ex-soldier. I served this country for 20 years. If that sacrifice means anything to you, please help me and others like me to get the money together for hostel accommodation. We are currently homeless and live in a tent in these wintry conditions.

He waited and watched. We lowered our heads. We rendered him invisible. I felt for him, but also felt uncomfortable and cautious. We as an English society have ways by which veterans can find support for the trauma they have faced. The Royal British Legion raises a lot of money and mobilises so many who spend hours getting the red poppies ready, distributing the boxes, helping to organise the parades, coordinating with churches for the solemnity, and with supportive pubs for the rest. It is an occasion that involves monarchy, government, the military and the church. It is standard practice to pick up your red poppy, outside train stations or when you collect your groceries, and wear it with pride, with the words 'Lest we forget'. There is an expectation that we will remember.

The next morning, I received an email from my children's school saying that they were selling poppies in reception and supporting the Royal British Legion. It also said there were other versions available. My joy was immediately quelled when I realised they were not referring to other colour poppies, like white to commemorate all the dead civilians and the so-called enemies, or the black poppy to re-remind the mourners that black and brown people on European soil and across the world perished. No, the school meant other versions of the red poppy – wristbands and badges. Without question we go along with this. We are conditioned and we believe we owe the veterans. We personally and collectively owe them, men like the apparition on the train.[12]

Subsequent to this I took part in a very moving service in the church in which I worked, in Suburbia. It was a rededication of the parish War Memorial. I pushed to have it called the War and Peace Memorial but the sponsorship we received prohibited my attempt. There is a list of names of young men from the parish who lost their lives to war. One of my church-wardens hired one of the best stonemasons, Andy Chalk, who put heart and soul into his work. It was a sacred duty. She commissioned a beautiful list of their names. Our little group gathered around the Memorial and conducted a short service. There was a historian, clergy, a local government representative, our sponsors, as well as our parishioners. But there were others there too. As the service went on, the immediate vicinity grew pregnant with the presence of the dead. One of our wardens, Clare, then played the reveille on a 1941 bugle and in the brief stillness that followed, the dead walked among us for just a while. It was more than memory, there was an added density in the air. Then the sense of presence dissipated.

I donated to the Royal British Legion, and donned my red poppy partly because I had mislaid my Peace Pledge Union white poppy; and partly, to be honest, because I did not want to stand out more than I already did. The insight I have gained from my years in a traditional setting and playing a part in Remembrance Sunday showed me a side of the English mentality and spirituality which can be discounted or discredited. At those moments, with several hundred people standing in the road to pay their respects, some men and women dressed in original uniforms, the rigour and the precision and pageantry of the scouts, guides and other uniformed organisations, and the parading of veterans, is deeply moving. There is an invocation, a deep ritual, with standards raised, weapons gleaming, wreaths handled with the tenderness of a mother with a newborn, the Salvation Army brass band, the drumming, all building to this moment of encounter. There is some deep folk-religious well that bubbles to the surface, and men like the veteran on the train are transfigured. And why do we come out in droves, buying our red poppies and wristbands in schools? Because we feel we owe them something. We instinctively know that the man on the train would not survive without an organisation, some mobilisation, to help his sense of integration. Something that happened a long time ago historically still impacts the lives and chances of those who inherit that legacy, whether actual or spiritual descendants.

We voluntarily give because the past impacts the present and future, and we augment and try to give support where we can. Because we've been taught and conditioned by our peers, politicians, and the press, that we owe them something. They are 'our boys'! It is an English story and the English must take responsibility for those within it. Except that it is a world story and the dead who clustered around the Memorial in my old suburban parish were black and brown, women and children too. So why when the call for reparations has been made in the UK has it so often been scorned? Millions upon millions of enslaved Africans laboured, were tortured and died for the national interest. And how many of the slaves' descendants serve and are members of the national church? Have the British public been conditioned that they owe these descendants nothing? 'The past is in the past.' A counter-message to that which we receive at a remembrance parade. The opposite message from that which I share as a priest when I divide the host and tip the cup, when I am saying 'When all blood is spilled and all bodies are broken, we should always see those moments as reaching forward and backwards in time.' Slavery is not seen as the English story any more; the monarchy, the government, the national church, and our education institutions do not want to look at what seems disconnected and distant. So much so, that when someone seeks to draw our attention to slavery it seems odd or wrong.

A new wave

A black priest, Canon Eve Pitts, was reported in the BBC news as wearing chains in her church in order to actively remember our enslaved forefathers and mothers. The action could seem odd, if not macabre.[13] Yet during remembrance white soldiers are made into heroes of valour, so why should black slaves be exorcised from our collective memories?

I tracked Canon Eve down. We initially spoke on the phone. She said, 'Are you sure you want to talk to me, I am quite unconventional?' In an era of the church's life where conventional is not working, maybe we need an alternative approach. Since our interview, I have discovered the range of challenges she has had to face, which gives even more power to the way she has overcome. Canon Eve has faced racism and sexism. As a woman and a person of colour she has a double set of oppressions to tackle. bell hooks,[14] a black academic, feminist and activist, points out how much conversation about blackness is disproportionately based around the black male story, and themes of femininity are based almost entirely on a white woman's set of oppressions. In the late 1950s and early 1960s my mother worked for one of the country's largest clothing and tailoring empires, Hepworths, at the Leeds branch. She faced racism there. She would sit on the long bench with the other white female machinists. Slowly but deliberately they would conspire to shove her off the work bench by gradually shifting down until they got her to the edge of the bench, and laugh as she would topple off. This was a popular game for them. Women of colour can have their particularity shoved off the end of the bench on a regular basis. They cannot trust the unconsidered white feminist narrative to represent or even recognise their own realities. As a black man this is my myopia too, and I am grateful to those like Natasha Beloved who have invited me as a black male not to succumb to the temptation of being the centre around which other people of colour orbit. bell hooks says about black women who fell between the stools:

> Other black women found themselves in limbo, not want-
> ing to ally themselves with sexist black men or racist white
> women. That black women did not collectively rally against
> the exclusion of our interests by both groups was an indication
> that sexist-racist socialization had effectively brainwashed
> us to feel that our interests were not worth fighting for, to
> believe that the only option available to us was submission
> to the terms of others. We did not challenge, question, or
> critique; we reacted.[15]

Women of colour, and those who identify as women of colour, have a voice to be heard and a viewpoint to be adopted. My interview with Eve Pitts shows what happens when someone stops reacting and begins to rewrite the terms. She has deter-mined to honour those who have gone before us in time, but who stand before us in space. Oh, and she has a thing about water. Here is the interview I had in a John Lewis department store in Birmingham with Canon Eve Pitts, one of Britain's first black woman priests:

Me   What was your introduction to the concept of Ancestors?

Eve   OK, I went on a cruise. While standing at the side of this enormous ship I was wondering why I really was on it. I was never comfortable with the sea. The sea represents to me the death of my ancestors and I stood there and I'm sure the sea spoke to me through a wave. The wave was strong and terrifyingly majestic and I remember thinking 'I don't want to come on a cruise again'. I felt a strong sense of their [the ancestors] presence. I've never been able to look at the sea without thinking about my ancestors, that experience helped me to crystallise my own thinking about the unrecognised graveyard of our ancestors. I have in my study at least five model slave ships.

Me   Tell me about the origin of the Ancestors Arise Service?

Eve   From that experience on the ship. The sense of the presence of the ancestors wasn't in my imagination. I thought, 'This isn't very Anglican.' I was brought up in an Anglican setting where the dead must be left alone, there is no connection between the living and the dead. Yet I was experiencing a real sense of my ancestors being around me and that led me to ask if I can feel that connection with my own ancestors, like my grandmother and grandfather, then the spirit of the rest of the dead of our people must be there too. In November we can have British society talking about their ancestors who have died in the war, what stops us from creating the space for our ancestors? How can we honour them?

Me   Your ministry feels more African in form and worldview, is that something you came in with intentionally or is that something which grew over time?

Eve   From as far back as I can remember I was always very African-centred, I didn't have to struggle for that, there were things that weren't making sense to me when I was a young priest. I remember thinking if I am going to embrace my ancestry then I have to embrace an African worldview, if I have to lose that heritage I dishonour my ancestors. The more I encountered the pain of Caribbean people, the more I knew that something about us must be put right, something spiritual needs to be put right if we are to find peace. The Anglican Church certainly hasn't brought black people peace. Not the people that I encounter, they display every level of self-hatred that you could think of.

Me   I'm curious about some of the resistance or challenge you've had, and how you have dealt with that. So, for example, people might say 'Well, if a white family comes to your church, will they feel that they are excluded', if so how would you address that?

Eve   Well we know about exclusion don't we! We don't want to upset those who are here, these nice Christians who are here, so please don't come! You know this struggle, this struggle for liberation, is not just about black people being liberated. If they are interested in a God who is just and fair then they won't have a problem because their history is mine and my history is theirs.

Me   And so you indicated that there is a sense of dis-ease with Anglicanism as it currently is. I wonder do you stay because of a sense of continued calling?

Eve   I believe I stay where I am to challenge the status quo. To challenge the cold, unacknowledged racism that still exists within the church. On the very first Ancestors Arise Service there were over a thousand people, and I have to say that I didn't think it was going to work at all ... I was humbled. On the way out someone said something really interesting. He said 'You are going to have to be protected, someone to protect you.' I said 'What from?' He said 'From all the forces out there that will attack you, and that also means the church.' You know I didn't take that very seriously at the time, it is a very lonely journey, but that is just the nature of the beast. If you are in it to be comfortable, if you are doing it because you want to be safe, then it is the wrong place to be.

Me   When black clergy, or those who want to become priests, seek you out, how would you prepare them?

Eve   I say, 'Know thyself.' Unless you know your cultural context, you become potentially a pawn in the chessboard in the way we function within the structures of the church. And one of the things I always say to young black priests is do not remove yourself from your cultural place because if you do, and you are unfortunate enough to get chewed up by the system, you have nothing to go back to.

Me   If there were some openness within the Bishops' Synod, the people who pull the strings ...

Eve   It's in their interests, because this rocky ship is sinking. We are in trouble, the Church of England is in trouble, they know that. It's in their interests for humanity, for the sake of their own humanity, for the humanity of British society, the church needs to begin to look at its structures and to redeem them, and to face the fact that if you are living in a pigsty, no matter how clean it looks, it's a pigsty, if you are living with the mess of history no amount of sanitisation is going to change that. It will be in the best interests of all of us if the church begins to speak the truth. When the truth is spoken, all of us will be in a better position. I said in a recent school assembly I spoke at that 'the dehumanisation of one group dehumanises all of us', and I said to the children 'You may not understand that now but you will get it', because the theme was 'To treat others as you would treat yourself'. The church hasn't acknowledged that yet, when that is acknowledged then that will save the church.

Notes

1 Dayfoot, A. (1999), *The Shaping of the West Indian Church 1492–1962*, Barbados: The Press, University of the West Indies, p. 88.

2 Hood, R. (1994), *Begrimed and Black*, Minneapolis: Fortress Press, p. 118.

3 Washington, J. (1984), *Anti-Blackness in English Religion 1500–1800*, New York: The Edwin Mellen Press, p. 400.

4 Ibid.

5 Ibid.

6 Ibid.

7 Gibson, Edmund (1727/1729), Two letters of the Lord Bishop of London, in David Humphreys, *An historical account of the incorporated Society for the Propagation of the Gospel in Foreign Parts*, London, 1730; facs. New York, 1969, pp. 265–6, as quoted in Dayfoot, A. (2000), *The Shaping of the West Indian Church 1492–1962*, Barbados, The Press University of the West Indies, p. 88.

8 Washington, *Anti-Blackness*, p. 509.

9 Ibid.

10 Collins, A. (2001), *Stories Behind the Best Loved Songs at Christmas*, Grand Rapids: Zondervan, p. 132.

11 Kohima Epitaph, Circa WWI by John Maxwell Edmonds (1875–1958).

12 http://vfpuk.org/articles/never-again-the-poppy-brand/.

13 www.bbc.co.uk/news/av/uk-england-birmingham-37363959/black-priest-walks-in-slave-chains-to-promote-remembrance.

14 bell hooks deliberately chooses to not capitalise her pen name, so that the focus is on her work not on her.

15 hooks, bell (2015), *Ain't I a Woman*, Abingdon: Routledge, p. 9.

3

No Pain Allowed

Can you recall a time when you felt excluded/intimidated because of your race and ethnicity within a predominantly white Christian context?

Experience of explicit racism was more common in my early experience of engagement with majority white churches. I've seen explicit expressions of exclusion as a lay person. As an ordained person, it has often been experienced in people's refusal to receive my ministry on account of my ethnicity. One more common experience is the assumption of deficit as a starting point from a good number of white people I've interacted with in ministry.

This happens regularly at clergy meetings. When I step into a room that feels more like a white middle-class boys' club than a gathering of church leaders. I always have to check myself, because there is a natural social pressure to assimilate with those in the room. So I tone down my blackness, and leave some of it at the door. Very seldom do I feel, as a black man, that I belong at such gatherings.

Yes, every two years at the diocesan clergy conference.

At a Men's Breakfast with elderly white men (this century). The room went silent when I walked in. Some people avoided eye contact. One man said to me, 'I left London because of all the Blacks.' Another said, 'It was wonderful when we had the empire, they were wonderful days, I loved India and the

Indians, we worked together on the ships and we worked well in civilising the Africans ...'

When I first started going to my current church I felt I didn't fit in; the music, the accents and the lack of diversity made me feel that. However I would say that I don't recall anyone in particular making me feel unwelcome and this was an adjustment I had to make. Now it feels very much like home!

The ADO [Area Director of Ordinands – like a careers officer] whom I was first assigned to, dismissed my calling describing it then as unrealistic. After a period of waiting I was reassigned to another ADO. The interesting thing is that in college I discovered two other ordinands of colour who had similar experiences in the hands of the same racist ADO! As I write today, he is still 'respected' within the diocese and remains unchallenged.

As a minority within the spaces I enter into, this is commonplace. What fits the description in the question is the moments when I'm called upon to justify a 'white' perspective in the discourse on race. There is a general lack of awareness as to how intimidating being a minority is in a space that could reject you for who you essentially are.

Studying in Oxford was a privilege, but I was reminded of the fact of being a brown person again and again. Either by being ignored by the tutors when trying to make a comment, or told by fellow students that I obviously did not understand some of the things taught.

The entire time of seminary. Especially when your seminary has only three BAME out of 40+, and then with graduating/ ordination, where there is only one.

I would say the music can make me feel excluded because it is not instinctively black. I miss this about my church, as music can be a key connecting point for black people in their spirituality.

At a healing service where I was preaching, a parishioner expressed afterwards how amazing it was that a negro was in training. He also felt it was appropriate to be tactile (taking hold of my hand). In short, I informed the priest (it was a residential placement), keeping the person anonymous, then to be informed that they knew who it was as they have a history! Enduring racially charged language publicly and privately (the hosts were even worse), I had no safe space, and the priest realised they had let me down pastorally.

* * *

The chord of peace was still resonating at the Quaker meeting. I turned to the woman sitting beside me and smiled as we exchanged handshakes. I used my voice for the first time in an hour. I had had a precious hour to clear my mind and deepen my perspective, held in the communal and gentle focus of others. I try to attend a Quaker meeting on a Sunday off once or twice a year. However, this meeting had been infiltrated. I had spotted another Church of England clergy person. I approached him shaking his hand with a conspiratorial wink indicating that we had both defected at least for the morning. I knew him, he was an acquaintance of mine. He was sitting beside an older white man who at that point seemed fairly harmless; I hadn't even realised they were together. I notionally acknowledged the man beside him and began to move towards the door and the promise of hot drinks and a cheeky cookie.

My friend called me back to say he wanted to introduce me to his friend, the gentleman who'd been sitting beside him. Well his friend was none other than: 'Retired Bishop Such and Such', who seemed pleased to have been introduced, and to my horror began to ask the standard bishopy questions, with a slight deliberative affectation of the voice: 'Where is your parish?' 'How is it all going?' I half expected him to complete his questions with 'dear boy'. Then alarm bells rang when I sensed he expected me to be an appreciative audience. He began to reflect back on his own ministry to offer fatherly advice. The chord of peace was being replaced by someone blowing their own trumpet. I wasn't in the mood for an unsolicited pep talk, so blurted out: 'I'm writing a book!' It did the trick of jarring the conversation, in effect I yanked the handbrake on his soliloquy. I was glad when he asked what the book was about. I replied, 'It is about my experience of being a clergy person from a minority ethnic background.' Retired Bishop Such and Such was ready with an answer, 'I hope you've got something positive to say, give us something positive!' I heard 'dear boy' in my head. I replied, 'I am sad to say there appears to be an old template of ministry and if one doesn't fit within that template it is difficult to flourish. A number of my black and minority ethnic colleagues are suffering in silence. In fact, many of them don't feel safe to share their challenges related to race.'

I could tell I was losing him, he had mentally switched channel as he continued, 'I admit the church still has a way to go, but we have done well in accepting homosexuality, and we have four black bishops and a black archbishop! Don't let your anger, pain, sadness or lament clutter your writing. That way your book might gain greater acceptance, then perhaps you can bring your protest.' Was he telling me to not speak up on the pain?

I used to work in a church as the youth worker. It was a big church with an impressive cafe. It was back in the days when church coffee was mainly available in instant form. The cafe was in the church crypt and two huge catering tins of coffee sat on the shelf behind the counter. It was also back in the days when fairly traded coffee was an acquired taste. So the church used Nescafé, which as we all know is the Satan of coffees because of the Nestlé powdered milk controversies. A number of people were boycotting Nestlé products overall in society and a number of Christians were taking a stand. However, it was the vicar who chose the Nescafé coffee, prizing the superior taste and flavour.

His primary concern was 'Did he like it or not?' A number of activist-y types agitated for fairly traded coffee to become the norm, and for the vicar to ban all trace of evil Nescafé. After mounting pressure he consulted with various groups and sure enough the fairly traded coffee won the battle, and Nescafé was relegated as a thing of the past. Proud tins of fairly traded ethical coffee took the place of the wicked Nescafé tins. People were celebrating a victory over 'the man', glad the vicar was persuaded to get aboard the justice train and peace was restored. I even saw the vicar 'seemingly' enjoying a cup or two after the service.

The other story. The church coffee shop was managed by a lovely lady from the West Indies, and she and I struck up a 'it's really nice to have someone else of colour to see from time to time' friendship. One afternoon, long after Nescafé-gate was a thing of the past, she pulled me aside after a staff meeting and told me the following tale. 'The vicar was getting hassled by xxx to change the coffee which he enjoyed to another brand which was more ethical but not as nice, in his mind.' I was beginning to check out, I knew this story, then she dropped the mic. 'I found the vicar in the kitchen one day emptying the large tins of fairly traded coffee into the bins. He spotted me and swore me to secrecy. He then tipped Nescafé into the fairly traded tins and then disposed of the Nescafé tins.' She chuckled to herself, glad to have unburdened herself of her secret. Which you, beloved reader, know now, many years later ... the vicar put no such injunction on me.

Bishop Such and Such, like this naughty vicar I've described, is wanting to tip me up and pour out all of my lament, pain, sadness, and anger into the kitchen bin. He will mop his brow and pour in hope, pleasantry and lots of status quo. I will look the same on the outside, with my contents displaced. The container and the contents do not always match. We could have a full complement of Black and Asian Minority Ethnic bishops but if they are ingloriously tipped out and filled up with something that suits the taste preferences of the dominant power, what you see is not what you get. If in theological and ministry formation they have been set on a particular path, if in their reading and form of leading they have been encouraged to empty themselves of what they already know and who they already are, everyone keeps the peace – but at what cost?

Nescafé represents an attitude of white superiority. A subjugation and minimising of what was. Its story and contents are now hidden in the other containers. If the fairly traded coffee represents clergy of colour, the activists will stop agitating, feeling they have been listened to, and that justice has been done. The ethical coffee contains a story, a journey, of ensuring fair, sustainable and equitable outcomes for all involved in the process. There have been negotiations, legislation, holding governments to account, and a focus on the producers and their contexts being honoured. But that story was disposed of because it is not to the taste of those in power, the bitter aftertaste makes them retch. Only the vicar was the winner in this instance. He tricked the activists into complacency, he called his worker into complicity, and to my mind, unethical confidentiality. We, the wider congregation, were none the wiser, thinking the quality of fairly traded coffee had improved and proud of doing our bit as individuals and a church. Until people of colour are not only promoting the Church of England as is, but are producing the Church of England as it could be, the representation argument carries less weight. With Retired Bishop Such and Such just looking at the surface, so much is missed. I think another thing Retired Bishop Such and Such was saying is that it takes time for things to change. 'Yes, there is a long way to go but we are about evolution not revolution.' That is a common theme and usually comes from someone not experiencing the pain of the situation.

Ottobah Cugoano

Robert Bernasconi is a philosopher and researcher on philosophy and race. I contacted him and he helpfully described the approach of freed slave Ottobah Cugoano's book, *Thoughts and Sentiments on the Evil and Wicked Traffic of the Slavery and Commerce of the Human Species* (a snappy title), published in 1787. Cugoano travelled from modern-day Ghana as a slave to the West Indies. He was later brought to England and was released at 18 as the laws of ownership could not be applied in the UK.[1]

Bernasconi notes how some philosophers who opposed

slavery had their convictions dulled because of how the church was viewed as being tolerant of slavery. William Paley was a philosopher and vocal opponent of the slave trade. When he became Archdeacon of Carlisle the publication of his lectures had little about slavery. He would not rule it out, and instead argued that the trade should be slowed down. He is quoted in Bernasconi as saying: 'we do not aim at the emancipation of the slaves, in the British West-Indies, but only that the future importation of them, from Africa, may be prohibited'. A gradual slowing down of the trade, a gradualism.[2]

There is a West Indian saying: 'They that feel it, know it.' Unless you are going through the pain of something, how can you pronounce a gradual approach for those who are?

Cugoano's first edition of the book had the following dynamic themes: An immediate end to the slave trade, and an end of slavery, with strategies of how this could be done.[3] He even went as far as to say that slaves shouldn't wait to be freed, they should escape their slavery:

> If any man should buy another man ... and complete him to his service and slavery without agreement of that man to serve him, the enslaver is a robber it is as much the duty of a man who is robbed in that manner to get out of the hands of his enslaver.[4]

This bore the possibility of revolt and revolution and shifted the power dynamic from the slaver growing a conscience, to the enslaved growing in courage. It also challenged the legal status of slavery, and therefore challenged the law. The enslaved humans should not have to wait. Waiting has been so much of my narrative, a reality of which I have become increasingly aware. I want those white elites in the Church of England to make it right for me. Maybe the waiting is over. Listen to Martin Luther King:

> Then there is another cry. They say, 'Why don't you do it in a gradual manner?' Well, gradualism is little more than escapism and do-nothingism, which ends up in stand-stillism.

And so we must say, now is the time to make real the promises of democracy. Now is the time to transform this pending
national elegy into a creative psalm of brotherhood. Now is
the time to lift our nation. Now is the time to lift our nation
from the quicksands of racial injustice to the solid rock of
racial justice. Now is the time to get rid of segregation and
discrimination. Now is the time. And so this social revolution
taking place can be summarized in three little words. They
are not big words. One does not need an extensive vocabu-
lary to understand them. They are the words 'all', 'here', and
'now'. We want all of our rights, we want them here, and we
want them now.[5]

King's soaring oratory, his push against gradualism, seems to
backtrack a little as he asks the white elites to give him and the
black community what they deserve. What if they are unable
to? What if they feel as trapped in their narrative as we can feel
in ours? Perhaps we complain as a way to procrastinate, and
the do-nothingism is for people of colour to reckon with too?

Cugoano challenged neutrality, saying that unless the British
as a nation spoke out *against* the slave trade they were complicit in it.[6]

Every man in Great Britain [is] responsible, in some degree
for the slavery and oppression of Africans unless he speedily
rise up with abhorrence of it in his own judgement, and, to
avert evil, declare himself against it.[7]

There are no innocent bystanders once we are aware of injustice. We have to act for its cessation. He brought that challenge
more strongly to those with high status (ancestors of Retired
Bishop Such and Such) when he said:

Men of eminence and power – nobles and senators, clergymen, and every man in office and authority – must incur
a double load of guilt, not only that burden of guilt in the
oppression of the African strangers, but also in that of an
impending danger and ruin to their own country.[8]

Racial injustice is a majority problem not a minority problem. This is an important warning against gradualism. Suppressing a problem will exacerbate it, creating many more. Cugoano offers an economic argument, advising that slaves should become paid labourers but that the new voluntary labour force would produce so much sugar, for reward as humans instead of repression as beasts. He states:

> And if Africans were dealt with in a friendly manner, a fruitful trade could develop which would soon bring more revenue in a righteous way to the British nation, than ten times its share in all the profits that slavery can produce.[9]

* * *

When we read scripture it is helpful to keep in mind the content we read, the context of the author, and the contemporary concerns of the interpreter, in this case myself. These perspectives form the coloured gels that lie on top of the light of the scripture. Then, as the colours overlap, a new colour is experienced. In the Gospel of Luke we come across an extreme tale of Jesus' encounter with a man possessed by demons in Gerasa. This man lived in the tombs. This man, we learn from the parallel in Mark's Gospel, threw stones at himself. This man is chained, except when he is not. On occasion he breaks free from his chains and terrifies those in the vicinity until he is subdued again. He is incarcerated, he self-harms, he is distressed. However the demons are understood today – spiritual or material or some combination of the two – the mental fragility and social ostracism are clear. But let's not forget the context of the author. The author was writing this around AD 70 according to many estimates. So there is at least a double vision of contemporary events of the author's time as well as the author recounting the Jesus story.

I read this story as a healing story, which offers the power of the mystical Jesus to heal the victims of the recent slaughter of the Jewish war, as much as it remembers the material Jesus healing the one man full of demons. Around the time

Luke was written, Gerasa was very much in the news with the Jewish–Roman war. Gerasa was one of the places where the revolt against Rome burned most brightly. The embers died down to reveal a thousand young men slain by Rome's military machine. Other young men, better armed and resourced, enacted state violence against those who were enacting street violence. Homes were burned and women and children were displaced and left in distress. The tombs were crowded, overflowing with the newly dead, leaving a region full of the undead and the not-quite-alive. Within this larger movement of imperial reassertion of power was the church narrative of persecution and binding and torture. Could it be that some of the power of this demoniac story lies less in its history but more in the collective trauma and memory of the people of this region? As this story is penned, might this man in the tombs be a totem enraged and empowered by the pain of the slaughter of men like him?

Cugoano had another strand to his argument, that of 'divine vengeance' if things did not change. This paralleled the white abolitionist Granville Sharp but differed in that Sharp did not see slave revolts as an aspect of God's judgement, whereas Cugoano, it could be argued, did:

> the voice of our complaint implies a vengeance because of the great inequity that you have done and because of the cruel injustice done unto us Africans.

Bernasconi demonstrates how Cugoano's argument goes a step further still, by suggesting that perhaps it was legitimate for the slavers themselves to be enslaved. A total reversal of the power arrangement. A true *Trading Places*.[10]

This is not inevitable, as Cugoano states:

> What revolution the end of that predominant evil of slavery and oppression may produce, whether the wise and considerate will surrender and give it up, and make restitution for the injuries that they have already done, as far as they can ...

Perhaps an invitation for white Britons to give up the benefits of power and privilege over others and a plea for reparations within the possibility and capacity of the nation. This is the ideal. Cugoano continues:

> or whether the force of their wickedness, and the iniquity of their power, will lead them on until some universal calamity burst forth against the abandoned carriers of it in, and against the crimes of nations in confederacy with them, is not for me to determine. But this must appear evident ... that these are crimes of the greatest magnitude, and a most daring violation of the laws and commandments of the Most High, and which, at last, will be evidenced in the destruction and overthrow of all the transgressors.

I am a believer, on good grounds, that the phrase the 'wrath of God' can be understood as shorthand for describing the consequences we bring upon ourselves by our sin, collective and individual. Cugoano speaks of a hardening of sin and a worsening of one's bad behaviour. Instead of surrender, confession and reparation, we lie, hide and cover our crimes but we end up cursed forever, trapped and enslaved.

When the second edition of Cugoano's book came out, he had stripped out all of those themes. Some say the response he got from his white readers led him to removing the more polemical and prophetic elements of his work.

A couple of hundred years later Martin Luther King threatened the same sense of possible revolt.

> But now more than ever before, America is forced to grapple with this problem, for the shape of the world today does not afford us the luxury of an anaemic democracy. The price that this nation must pay for the continued oppression and exploitation of the Negro or any other minority group is the price of its own destruction. For the hour is late. The clock of destiny is ticking out, and we must act now before it is too late.[11]

In this I see that Martin and his community are acting. Who is the 'we' he is appealing too? Who is he asking to take responsibility for the negroes' plight? Are white and black people siblings? The Hebrew Scriptures tell the story of the first murder and the introduction of physical violence into the world. One man called Cain kills his brother Abel. The passage reads like this:

> Now Cain said to his brother Abel, 'Let's go out to the field.' While they were in the field, Cain attacked his brother Abel and killed him.
>
> Then the Lord said to Cain, 'Where is your brother Abel?' 'I don't know,' he replied. 'Am I my brother's keeper?' The Lord said, 'What have you done? Listen! Your brother's blood cries out to me from the ground. Now you are under a curse and driven from the ground, which opened its mouth to receive your brother's blood from your hand.' (Gen. 4.1–10)

If the notion of the ground having a mouth to receive the slain is not horrifying enough, that the spilled blood is able to vocalise its victimhood and name the perpetrator should make every would-be murderer shudder. In Geresa there was a lot of blood crying out. I imagine it was deafening. I think a man possessed by demons hanging around the tombs becomes entirely understandable.

His chains are physical and psychological. When he breaks free from the chains he is still welded and melded to his demons. It is into this context that Jesus arrives. I suggest the healing of this one fractured man is also a prayer for the healing of a broken society. Jesus addresses the man who is host for the demons that declare their name as Legion. The political punch of this nomenclature is hard to miss. Legion was the group of Roman soldiers, it was a legion that slaughtered the thousand young men. The division deployed to crush the rebellion had pigs on their shields. The Roman armies are Cain exacting violence on those in Geresa, who are Abel.

The transatlantic slave trade elevated one brother, Cain the white, over his brother Abel, the one of colour. When God says to Cain 'Where is your brother?' he shrugs his shoulders and says 'I don't know. Am I my brother's keeper?' Did the Roman army crushing the rebellion have common feeling with the young men they butchered? The imprint of this terror was imprinted upon and within the tomb dweller.

When talk of reparation comes up (if it comes up at all), do white senior clergy have any sense of how to answer the question God is asking (and if God isn't asking it, then God's own people *are* asking it)?

'Cain, where is your brother?'

There have been over three decades of failure to adequately answer this question with anything other than a shoulder shrug. Those in the (Club) are saying: 'I don't know, am I my brother's keeper?' Maybe yes, maybe no, but if we are not fighting injustice, we are complicit with our brothers' and sisters' deaths, social, spiritual and societal. With mass incarceration, stop and search, hurdle after hurdle to get access to education, opportunities in the jobs market and decent housing, and a woefully low access to its own church leadership, the roar of blood is crying out. No wonder black mental health is among the worst of all groups in British society.[12] No wonder black people feel the least welcome in communities,[13] no wonder they get heavier sentences. We are Abel. We are overwhelmed by Legion. We need to be free. But it will cost. In the Gerasa story, Jesus addresses the demons. They do not want to be banished when, in effect, Jesus sends them to their room. They ask to be allowed to enter grazing pigs nearby. There is a huge commotion as the pigs squeal, infected by the destructive spirits, and race headlong over a cliff, plummeting to their deaths. Some buildings will be sold, some land will be repurposed, some accounts will be liquidated, the death of the pigs was the collapse of an entire industry for that town.[14]

The miracle ruined the economy. Ending slavery challenged the British economy. The slave owners, not the enslaved, had a bailout that was second only to the 2008 bank crash bailout and was only fully paid back during the last decade. How can the white senior leaders in the Church of England play their part in healing black trauma? Certainly not while they retain white power and privilege. The clues come in Galatians, by becoming 'a slave to the slaves'. What would it do for Cains to become a slave to Abels? To truly commit, at the expense of your freedom, to a cause that takes your money and your life. The work of repair. Not the warning of Cugoano, but a voluntary admission of taking initiative and responsibility. A patchwork blanket of multiple parts designed to cover the nakedness of the tomb dwellers. What does this look like? In the UK, a number of white senior figures in the Church of England have their fingers firmly in their ears to ignore the cries. In the Episcopal Church in the USA they have been on this journey for a lot longer. In November 2019 I read this on the website of the Diocese of Long Island:

Diocese of Long Island Designates Funds for Reparations and Relief Efforts

November 20 2019

The Right Revd Lawrence C. Provenzano, Bishop of Long Island, announced at the diocesan convention on November 16 that an estimated half-million dollars from the pending sale of the former St. Matthias Church property in Wantagh will be reserved for a plan of reparations. In this action, the diocese joins with a growing number of dioceses and entities across the Episcopal Church in acknowledging their roles during the period of slavery in the United States. The bishop said this will 'be the start of a reparations fund to be held by the trustees of the diocese and administered by an appointed committee of Diocesan Council, the income from which will be distributed in the form of scholarships and incentives to minority young adults seeking opportunity in education and business within the geography of our diocese.'

> And we have been able to contribute $50,000 to Cod-
> rington College in Barbados, a theological seminary that
> serves the Province of the West Indies. The seminary has
> been in urgent need of support for its faculty and this is
> one way for us to provide a thank offering for many of our
> clergy whose theological education and formation began at
> Codrington College.

This seems light years away from what I could imagine the
church doing in the UK. It begins with acknowledgement.
Some I have spoken with have stated how they want to be
heard when they share their pain. It puts me in mind of the
Truth and Reconciliation Commission held in South Africa.
Could that be a methodology for harvesting the stories? I
asked a group of black and brown people 'What message do
you have for the Archbishop of Canterbury?' They said 'We
would ensure he heard our stories.' Would that be enough?
Do we actually need a Truth and *Reparations* Commission?
With some promise of restitution. I spoke earlier about Retired
Bishop Such and Such, but we are not quite finished with him
yet. I write tough, but in the sedate foyer of the peace-warrior
Quakers I nodded along, smiled and said 'Thank you Bishop.
Keep me in your prayers.' I took and shook his hand and began
to move off, when his invisible mask/mitre slipped. There was
a distant sound of squealing as he began to talk again; he
was sounding less certain, but making more sense. After the
squeals came the splash of the drowning livestock. The retired
bishop brought his thumbs and forefingers together to form
a pyramid. He was speaking to no one in particular, saying
'You know, I think the pyramid needs to be inverted.' He spun
his forefingers downwards inverting the shape. He continued
speaking as if he were another man, saying: 'I haven't really
taken many risks through my ministry, and I regret that.'
   There was none of the former self-assurance but instead
there was an honest reflection and an accompanying sense of
powerlessness. I shook his hand again, saying, 'Perhaps your

ministry isn't quite over yet.' The Quaker meeting had acted as a demilitarised zone, neutral territory for clergy at opposite ends of the ecclesiastical church ladder to meet. The power dynamics, and what and who was privileged, were altered. As he flipped the point of the pyramid downwards he demoted his own sense of status and I felt for the first time we were peers, and that he might be able to hear me, and I him. It was a beginning. Then we went our separate ways. Maybe bishops, retired or otherwise, may take courage and learn from others how to create a church for all to flourish. Where we can be our brothers' and sisters' keepers, supporters and friends.

Notes

1 Bernasconi, R. (2018), 'Ottobah Cugoano's place in the history of political philosophy', in George Hull, *Debating African Philosophy: perspectives identity, decolonial ethics and comparative philosophy*, London: Routledge, p. 27.

2 Bernasconi, 'Ottobah', p. 32.

3 Ibid., p. 34.

4 Fryer, P. (1984), *Staying Power: The History of Black People in Britain*, London: Pluto Press, p. 99.

5 King, Martin Luther Jr (1963), Address at the Freedom Rally, Cobo Hall, Detroit, Michigan. Stanford University, The Martin Luther King Jr Research and Education Institute.

6 Bernasconi, Ottobah, p. 35.

7 Fryer, *Staying Power*, p. 99.

8 Ibid.

9 Ibid., p. 100.

10 Bernasconi, 'Ottobah', p. 36.

11 Address at the Freedom Rally in Cobo Hall.

12 Pinto, R., M. Ashworth and R. Jones (2008), 'Schizophrenia in black Caribbeans living in the UK; an exploration of underlying causes of the high incidence rate', *British Journal of General Practice* 58 (551): 429. Especially for black Caribbeans, there is a nine times greater risk of black people of West Indian heritage becoming schizophrenic than for a white contemporary. The next category at highest risk are black Africans. Taking out the hereditary links and cannabis use, Pinto et al. have outlined a number of probable causes. One factor considered is migration. The assumption is that once a generation has gone by, the

descendants become assimilated into their new communities. However, in the case of the black Caribbean the risk of schizophrenia grows in successive generations. This is not the same when comparing them to their Asian contemporaries. So social factors are considered. Sociologists refer to the term 'social capital', described in the report as 'the glue that holds society together' and 'social cohesion'; the absence of a father figure in particular is higher in the black Caribbean population than the white British population. These factors are both seen to play a part. In South Asian families the close ties help mitigate against schizophrenia. The report states:

> African-Caribbeans living in predominantly white neighborhoods have been found to have a higher incidence of schizophrenia ... Individuals living in areas where their own ethnic group constitutes a smaller proportion of the local population have been reported to feel excluded from local social networks.

13 https://assets.publishing.service.gov.uk/government/uploads/system/uploads/attachment_data/file/686071/Revised_RDA_report_March_2018.pdf, p 16.

14 Myers, C. (2008), *Binding the Strong Man*, Maryknoll, NY: Orbis Books. The discussion in this book is cross-disciplinary and very engaging, rooting the story in the social, economic and political realities.

4

Slave Ship

If you've felt discrimination or encountered prejudicial attitudes, would you report it to senior white leadership? If not why not? And if not, is there anywhere else you'd take it?

These are comments from black and brown clergy and laity from seven dioceses, including male and female voices who wish to remain anonymous.

> I spoke with the bishop's chaplain about my concerns, and of the undue pressure I felt from the bishop. The bishop's chaplain was meant to be my chaplain too. He seemed intimidated by the bishop, and reluctant to help. Realising he was unwilling or unable to support I asked who I could complain to, or mention the bullying I felt from the bishop. The bishop's chaplain could not suggest a single person I could turn to. He refused to help. I spoke with another senior figure in the diocese who said of the bishop 'We work together, you can't play us off against each other.' I was devastated. I was not intending to play people off against each other I just wanted to understand who could support me in my plight.

> I tend to challenge racist behaviour and call it out as much as possible. Report mechanisms don't seem to be clear. Besides, our church does not have a good record in condemning and challenging racist behaviour. Furthermore, most BAME people do not trust the institution's ability to understand the subtle nuances of racism that we are subjected to on a daily basis. From experience, I know many BAME people who choose not to make a fuss so that they do not end up with labels such as 'troublemaker'.

I have felt discrimination in the church and reported it more than once. I am normally treated a bit like a nuisance, and like I had a chip on my shoulder, or am trying to play the 'race card'. The normal response I have experienced is one of white fragility.

I have been seen as someone challenging unconscious white norms, and treated as a threat ... To report something so personal puts me in a position of vulnerability, and leaves me open to all sorts of labels and tropes. If I am going to report something such as a racial violation, I need to truly trust the person I am reporting to. Nowadays, due to past experiences, that kind of trust does not come to me easily.

No, I think it would cause more unrest, and senior leadership would have no idea in how to address it without making things worse. I would discuss it with fellow BAME clergy, but there are very few around.

I wouldn't necessarily report it because I tend to deal with these matters by assessing whether the outcome would result in a positive one.

Initially no, as I had accepted my 'place' and also feared I would be blacklisted; but now definitely yes as I have a better understanding of the law, my rights and the C of E BAME.

I'd report it to a senior white leader, yes. Then again all our leaders are white so I'd have no other choice.

The processes that currently exist to report incidents require a victim to meet someone who resembles the perpetrator. This is not a conducive environment for reporting incidents and has ensured – in my case – that I haven't reported any incidents that do not meet a certain threshold. This is be-cause many of these incidents have been deemed 'minor' by those in authority over me, making light of the gravity of my experience as the victim.

As a black man, I'm required to be tougher without it being recognised that the weight is already heavier, purely because of my difference from the dominant ethnicity and culture. I have to face otherness without complaint, ignorance without complaint, and can only bring an issue up when it is a wilful act of discrimination. This is too high a threshold for the bulk of the difficult attitudes I face.

I did not during training at all – I was scared. Church is a grapevine and people talk. I did raise it post-training with the DDO [Diocesan Director of Ordinands]. The response was silence.

No, I would not report it. This is not to suggest the senior white leadership does not care about racism and prejudice, but there is a lack of knowledge/comfort on how to deal with discrimination. Additionally, some senior white leadership have commented that the encounters 'are not really racist'.

I have during training on two occasions and the outcome remains obscure. For the other times, I have referred to my support network and spiritual directors. I no longer trust the system and I understand that it is within my best interest to remain silent.

* * *

Martin Luther King said:

I know we have heard a lot of cries saying, 'Slow up and cool off.' We still hear these cries. They are telling us over and over again that you're pushing things too fast, and so they're saying, 'Cool off.' Well, the only answer that we can give to that is that we've cooled off all too long, and that is the danger. There's always the danger if you cool off too much that you will end up in a deep freeze.[1]

People of colour battle against the harsh weather conditions of whiteness. White privilege offers arctic clothing to its members.

For the lucky ones, the cold becomes negligible, the whitened environment becomes pleasurable, and people of colour without such coverings become disposable. Poor whites and queer whites can also suffer; however, it may be easier for them to elicit empathy, the card-carriers seeing themselves in the mirror of their lives. People of colour are caught in a long winter. They have encountered Jadis, the spell-caster and bringer of winter from C. S. Lewis's The Chronicles of Narnia. Jadis has her white wolves around her feet, predators looking for lambs to devour. People of colour can be spellbound, ossified into organic tombs of stone, awaiting the wild lion's breath and roar to thaw them and transform the environment so they can remain warm, and summer can finally arrive as they become fully alive. But Aslan hasn't been seen for a long time in this country, or in its ports or borders. There is a rumour of his return. It is said he can be heard in the dead of night – but it's more of an anguished scream than a roar. And who believes rumours any more?

In Aslan's absence, Jadis pretends to be the lion, roaming the Church of England's dioceses, parishes, primary schools, colleges and harbours. Often Aslan is on the recruitment poster attracting you into the harbour office. The majestic ship gleams ahead of you, with the image of Aslan proudly displayed on the masthead. To the alert travellers Jadis' silent white wolves in the near distance should be a portent. Imagine a throng of black and brown clergy hopefuls clustering to enter the harbour office. You are growing in excitement at the thought of the voyage into ministry and mission. Some white hopefuls are ahead of you in the queue and a few of the white cohort appear to take something from a little bowl offered by the woman in the booth. It is Jadis in the shadows. You arrive at the desk to buy your ticket unknowingly encountering Jadis, her voice bright, a bowl of Turkish Delight just out of sight. The bowl is not offered to you as these special pieces of Turkish Delight are for her prized white passengers – she has other plans for some of them. You sign in, and you do not realise as you write your name in her 'book' that you are putting yourself under her power and committing to a perilous journey.

Thinking you were following the way of the Cross, you unwittingly become subject to the way of the Crown:

> Enslaved people understood God as the Author and Source of freedom. They apprehended freedom as God's intention for them. Slaveholders tried to impose themselves between the slave and the God and, to this end, manipulated Christian teaching.[2]

When you work as a priest you are licensed by a diocese. As I mentioned earlier, there are 42 dioceses in the Church of England, regions overseen and led by a diocesan bishop. The cathedrals are often the port and portal into giving you your ticket and tools. Inside the church buildings are where you receive the blessing and benefits you need to effectively journey on board the diocesan ship, which promises to usher you and others to safe harbour. You are commissioned to collect passengers and crew and survive the storms, steered by a great captain, the bishop. But the cost of passage is greater than the price tag reveals. You have declared, you have signed and surrendered to what looks like Aslan sitting off in the middle distance near the altar. You are conducted through a vestry door which leads to the ship of this particular diocese. You miss seeing attendants gather round 'Aslan', roughly tugging at the mane which loosens and the full head mask is removed, revealing that the lookalike is actually one of Jadis' lackeys. You have been inducted into the wrong religion. Instead of a diocese, you have signed up to 'Dire-Seas'.

As a person of colour, you strangely begin to feel the cold, as winter begins its work on you. You hurry up the gangplank, shivering and scanning for others like you. As you board, you smile as you see your friends, the white priests, waving at you. They are wearing thick coats, woollens and gloves. You're in a t-shirt and shorts, but no one at this point seems to notice the disparity. At this point you are unaware you will be ushered below deck where there are no emergency exits or lifeboats. Once on board you are further required to fill in some more paperwork on your application before you can take a job on the ship. The last question on the form reads as follows:

Are you a member of any political party or institution which espouses racist values or ideals?[3]

As a person of colour, it is meant to reassure you that the ship you are boarding is safe and all the passengers and crew have been vetted. It is a stark question that one imagines is seeking to call out and denounce participation in anti-black and brown, dehumanising political parties, and membership of groups with dangerous ideologies. I assume someone worked hard to ensure that question was there, and I am grateful it is acknowledged. But I'm aware of the irony. The organisation that is asking if I am part of an organisation that espouses racist values or ideals is itself institutionally racist. And here is one of the problems.

The UK has different threat levels to determine the correct response to a potential terror attack. Here is where the multiverse kicks in. There are overlapping and divergent experiences in seemingly the same spaces.

Threat Level	Response
Critical	Exceptional
Severe	Heightened
Substantial	Heightened
Moderate	Normal
Low	Normal

Whereas the white passenger may start on a threat level of low to moderate and then, with the stresses and strains of ministry, whether by choice or circumstance, move to substantial, the person of colour may begin at threat level substantial, and move up regularly to severe and sometimes to critical.[4]

You stand huddled with your cohort for warmth on the deck, excited about Aslan's adventure, following the way of the Cross, unaware that the way of the Crown is slowly freezing you. That's when you hear an almost imperceptible murmur. You separate from the group as you are drawn by the sound, which appears to be coming from the sea. You peer over the rails, the lapping waves licking the side of the boat. You spot a large indiscernible shadow beneath you, as you detect the sound of sobs and muffled shouts coming from below the waves. You call the rest of the cohort over to see if they can hear it. They are shivering and wander over, and they hear it too. One of the officers spots you and orders a horn blast that snaps you all to attention, and you retreat from the water's edge. The warning of the drowned messengers goes unheeded.

If you train at a theological college, towards the end of your time you investigate where you can do your apprenticeship – your curacy. There are jobs advertised across the theological colleges and you begin your explorations. Often you might want to return to the diocese you left and to the bishop who sponsored the costs of your training. My diocese had a high-ranking bishop who, as well as governing and captaining the whole vessel, had personal charge of a slice of it, while the other slices were delegated to what are known as area or suffragan bishops, depending on where you are. I was keen to return to the city which sponsored me to train, but didn't see much in the classifieds doing the rounds. But not all jobs on offer make it to the classifieds. In my final year of training to become a Church of England minister, I was headhunted by a church. This church was a global faith enterprise, the Amazon of the Christian world, distributing goods and services in an ever-expanding, ever-ambitious march.

I thought this juggernaut church was acting with over-confidence by circumventing the assumed system of recruiting, so I mentioned to a member of the team a meeting I had coming up with the diocesan bishop. I mentioned this fact thinking that the church was under the authority of the bishop. I, in my little way, was trying to signal that I had friends in high places, I had the bishop's protection; so they had better look after me as we explored the possibility of ministry together. I was also wanting to indicate that I was exploring other options. They were not the only game in town. The bishop would come good and provide other options. I didn't know then that the bishop enjoyed shelter under *their* umbrella, and not the other way around. He was a minor celebrity at their annual conference, and his reputation as a bishop overseeing numerical growth in the church in large part came from having their active church revitalisation project in his backyard, as it were. My fixer from the church did not skip a beat. He simply gave me instructions, my script for my forthcoming meeting with the bishop. I was to keep quiet about their approach. I hardly knew the people at this church but felt I was being drawn into a pact of silence. I felt uncomfortable with this polite demand. It was indicative of one of the many phrases I would hear once I was working there – when you want to get things done you 'love em and shove em'. The assumption being the it's in the best interest of the loved to be 'shoved' by the higher entity.

A few weeks later I had the meeting with the bishop. A moment came when he asked me about the sort of ministry I would like. I was honest with him, asking for a traditional parish ministry with enough structure for me to innovate within set lines, and a good vicar to train me. He stroked his chin, appearing to listen. That's the type of church I wanted but that was not what I was being offered. In my whole ministry so far I have been steered towards places and people by those in power offering me a very limited choice. What is called the discernment process is often a subtle shove towards a preordained outcome. There is an impression of freedom of choice, with churches A, B and C all in your sights. But the place you are standing is a slowly revolving disc, you do not realise you are moving, and it always brings you face to face with the magician's choice, which you now believe was your own. I did not know that then. I saw this meeting with the bishop as a bid for freedom from the popular and polished church. With the verbal NDA ringing in my ears I felt divided loyalty between the bishop, who'd been a benefactor of sorts, helping with some furnishings, supporting with funding for my dyslexia testing, and being generous once our firstborn came along with purchase of a needed mattress – and the shiny church which was an unknown entity. I chose to tell him about their interest in me. I was relieved I had picked a side. I was choosing the traditional church over the shiny Amazon-like powerhouse. I felt proud of my integrity, and I had demonstrated my allegiance to the bishop. I expected that that was the end of my conversations with said church. I thought the bishop would say 'Wise choice, let us consider these other options for a fine fellow such as yourself.' I was naive, and unaware of the unity of whiteness, the social capital that comes of a shared privileged heritage and dominant societal status.

My first surprise came when the bishop admitted he already knew of their interest. I was confused as to what this meant. I was not feeling entirely at peace with this ship I was being invited to join. It looked great from the outside, but as the first potential clergy person of colour they had ever had with a huge multicultural congregation, I had a quiet sense of dread. I thought I was dealing with two separate entities, but I was mistaken. There was and is a reality behind the buildings and the titles that held the white upper middle and upper classes together. Behind the curtain they were all sharing a dressing room. The bishop approved of the idea of this church. I realised he had thought this through, saying: 'We don't have the central funding to bring you back, but the church has the resources to provide a stipend [a form of salary and provision of housing] and get you back into the city.' He was handing me over to them – or was he selling me to them? What was I worth? I was not to be part of the central system of recompense. Instead, I would be on the church's payroll, and governed by their laws. I was a rare commodity in that I was a black man from the smallest nation in the Western Hemisphere operating in one of the most confident dioceses, in one of the most famous of its churches. So I realised the church occupied a place of power over and/or with the bishop; and their collective decisions would be over and against me. I went on to join the diocese and when ordained had these sentiments confirmed.

They [those being ordained] have duly taken the oath of allegiance to the Sovereign and the oath of canonical obedience to the Bishop. They have affirmed and declared their belief in the faith which is revealed in the Holy Scriptures and set forth in the catholic creeds and to which the historic formularies of the Church of England bear witness. (BB Canon C 15.1(1))

I took the oaths very seriously. Two bishops laid their hands on my head as I knelt before them. I have the picture. It symbolised surrender to the calling and to God, I wonder if it was me bending the knee to whiteness too.

There are a number of difficult instances I could recount but concerns from my publisher and my own sense of exposure prevent me saying more. On reflection, I now visualise a huge picture of the queen on her throne, with Prince Philip standing behind, dress sword softly glinting, subtly hinting. There was nowhere to hide. I am only too grateful for the support of an excellent therapist, wife and friends who buoyed me up at this time, one of many dark storms as I travelled on the Dire-Seas. The Church of England does have CMEAC (Committee for Minority Ethnic Anglican Concerns), and I *was* concerned, and had concerns, but was not aware it was for me. Now, when I look at the word, I perceive a prayer: 'C (see) **ME A**nglican Church'.

What could be the historical roots of this dread I felt? In the days of slavery there was an understanding of slavery as social death. M. Shawn Copeland documents the legal standing in parts of America where slaves were not allowed to speak against a white person in any court. They were not allowed to defend themselves when attacked.[5] This chapter opened with a list of statements by black and brown Anglicans, ordained and from a range of dioceses/dire-seas. I discussed the book with my publisher, stating what a poor employer the Church of England was to many people of colour. They requested that I found evidence to show this is not only my story. I tried, but found again and again people would say the following: 'Let me tell you this thing that happened to me – but don't put it in the book' or 'This is for your ears only.' Eventually I crafted a survey and offered anonymity and the truth and the pain flooded into my inbox. But this was the tip of the iceberg. There are others whose pain sits on paperwork in courtrooms, or is discussed in closed boards and committees. Sometimes years drag by as they seek justice but have to protect the predators. The white wolves have blood around their mouths – and it is not their own blood.

Anthony Reddie documents:

> Due to the effects of racialized oppression and marginali-
> sation, many black people may well be suspicious or even
> reluctant to talk in depth about personal stories or experi-
> ences. This reluctance is exacerbated if the person seeking to
> initiate or facilitate the conversation is a White European.[6]

My respondents to the survey are hyper aware of their token
status, and the ease with which they could be identified and
punished by white leaders in the church. Reddie is speaking of
black elders, but I feel the point stands for black and brown
people of all ages who, in his words, 'submerge or disguise
aspects of their existence and experience from the wider world
which is often dominated by white people'.[7]

But I doubt, even with evidence, that we will be believed
as the threat level for us is heightened so that the same room
throws up different experiences. If you are bereaved, a favourite piece of music of your loved one in a coffee shop can trigger
an immediate and visceral response. The music has a deeper
meaning and can take you unawares. Dan Hauge, a Critical
Whiteness thinker and one of a growing number of theologians
and thinkers on trauma, speaking of the black situation in
America says:

> The lack of sensitivity of black people's collective trauma
> is then compounded by the fact that the dominant culture
> consistently demands 'evidence' … to genuinely consider the
> overwhelming testimony of people of colour regarding the
> systemic nature of racism.[8]

Hauge goes on to discuss the environment and the many ways
one may encounter racism as a felt reality.[9] He spells out how
white people automatically minimise the narratives of people
of colour. An incident which may feel minor to a white person
could perpetuate the state of high alert in a person of colour
who is unaware of which cupboard or corridor the racism will
emerge from next.[10]

So, what do we do about this, people of colour? One response is we come together and find each other across our sectors and disciplines. One response in the 1800s was the Sons of Africa.

Sons of Africa

Ottobah Cugoano was a founding member of the Sons of Africa in 1787, seen as Britain's first black political group, which had black London leaders coming together to plan and prepare for purpose.

It was made up of those who had formerly been slaves or who had parents who had been slaves. They supported each other with their individual projects, and they embarked on collective projects together, adding their signatures to letters, speaking as a group. They were public figures. Cugoano and Olaudah Equiano were both published authors. They were also involved in arts and culture and they had political clout. From this base they also worked within other groups with willing whites who were supporters in the struggle.[11] I would love to be part of a movement like that, a sons and daughters of Africa.

One time I *was* nearly part of a movement like that. I hustled an invite to a small audience with Michael Curry, the head of the American Episcopal Church. It was held in an iconic home, the former home of John Collins. Nelson Mandela and Martin Luther King had both visited this place. Attached to a visit to a neighbouring cathedral, Michael was to meet with us and then head off to the mighty throng who would only see him as a speck in the distance. We, however, would be in touching distance of our big brother in the struggle. Was this my Sons of Africa moment? There was an impressive cast of academics, culture leaders, conscious clergy and political thinkers. This was my experience of walking into what I thought was a low-to-moderate threat environment and having to upgrade that assessment pretty quickly. BraveSlave penned the following account:

Quarantine

'It's all about love', said the potbellied
purple shirt wearing, ebony, smiley,
preacher primate.
The Royal Wedding preacher warmed my
inner climate.

Yet my hand is outstretched but
remains empty,
My hope was
outstretched but remains empty ...

Zoom in to that fateful afternoon,
witness me excited entering
the room.
He arrives and is marched upstairs
to meet his conversation partner,
He is quarantined away from us,
And I would rather, his time was spent,
was lent, to the waiting hopeful remnant.

The advance guard a white-right man,
comes to warm up the crowd explain the plan.
Ensure we are on the same page.
That's when I realise it is all staged.
And the director, producer,
lead actor is this white man,
An always 'right man' was the
wrong man for this night man.

From the very beginning he asserted control,
I'm an artist and I feel this stirring in my soul.
Something feels strange, it's all prearranged
and we have been edited out of this moment before
it has even begun. Beyond words is my grief
As I speak in tongues.

When we the people sit it becomes not one room but two,
an invisible partition, falls into position,
as this white-right man states the terms and conditions.

He wanted a Taskforce as a modern day Wilberforce,
He asked ' why are black people not ascended to the highest
positions of leadership?'

I answered 'when white men and right
men move out of the spotlight
take our lead, and join our fight, then ...'

But my lips were still. I had answered in my mind as I felt
    intimidated,
by the projection of his weakness as strength, my hope was
    incinerated,
He continued: 'Did we all want to be involved,
with this big problem he was fixing to solve?'

He then laid down the law as he
determined our activity,
feet firmly on the floor
he demanded our passivity.

He explained. Michael Curry is in a hurry.
But I knew he had been sequestered
above our heads. Thirty minutes
we had already waited, I grew frustrated,
He explained:
There will be no participation,
from the gathered congregation.
The Q and A within closed conversation.

If all that didn't seem too much,
he made another prohibition, this time no touch!
No touch was permitted we are told 'not to pounce'
After that one or two guests decided to bounce.

The people in the room could have been a movement,
but we will never know because we were instructed
not to move, Michael Curry could have held us,
blessed us, spoken comfort to our tribulation,
but he did not even hear our names ...

BraveSlave[12]

Notes

1 King, Martin Luther Jr (1963), Address at the Freedom Rally,
Cobo Hall, Detroit, Michigan. Stanford University: The Martin Luther
King Jr Research and Education Institute.

2 Copeland, M. Shawn (2010), *Enfleshing Freedom*, Minneapolis:
Fortress Press, p. 42.

3 The final question on the standard application form for a job in
the Church of England.

4 https://en.wikipedia.org/wiki/UK_Threat_Levels.

5 Copeland, *Enfleshing Freedom*.

6 Reddie, A. (2003) *Nobodies to Somebodies*, Peterborough: Epworth Press, p. 198.

7 Ibid.

8 Hague, Dan (2016), 'The trauma of racism and the distorted
white imagination', in *Post Traumatic Public Theology* by Stephanie N.
Areal and Shelly Rambo, London: Palgrave Macmillan, p. 94.

9 Ibid., p. 95.

10 Ibid.

11 Olusoga, D. (2016), *Black and British*, London: Macmillan. p. 212.

12 Unpublished collection.

Intermission: A conversation with Rose Hudson-Wilkin

The seeds of this book were sown in 2010 when I completed my MPhil degree. I had explored some of these themes in my thesis and one of the subjects of interview then was the Revd Rose Hudson-Wilkin. She was then a vicar in Hackney, which overlapped with being one of Her Majesty's Chaplains, before her role in parliament as chaplain to the Speaker of the House, before she was a friend of the young Royals, before she'd been on BBC Radio 4's *Woman's Hour* as a guest editor, or *Desert Island Discs*. Fast forward to May 2019. I met Rose at the Houses of Parliament before she became the Bishop of Dover. I attended her midday Eucharist and then we shared lunch. Throughout this ten-year ascension she has been absolutely consistent: bold, incisive, down to earth, no nonsense, quick to laugh, wise and offering one a place of safety. She arrived fully assembled from Jamaica. If you are born and raised here, there is more a sense of you being built with a mixture of parts in real time in the public eye. It was a pleasure to have a wide and free-ranging conversation with her then, and since her appointment she has remained her authentic, authoritative, accessible self.

Me   I'm curious, from your perspective, how does whiteness work here in the UK? How is racism expressed in contrast to places like South Africa or North America, where you can see it?

Rose   Yes, it's blatant there. I think it's much more covert here. When you say, 'How does whiteness work here?'

are you talking about 'here' in terms of parliament or just Britain?

Me   UK.

Rose   I think what you see is whiteness presented as normal, and if that is presented as normal then it means that I am not normal, you are not normal. It means that minority ethnic people are not normal. We're outside the frame of normality.

(My ten-year-old daughter stood over my shoulder when I was reading through this interview and she said we don't need to fit in the frame, we need a bigger frame.)

One of the challenges and the problems here is that whiteness occupies all that space and anything outside the space they don't treat with the same respect, with the same dignity as they would themselves. They have fears that we're not going to be good enough. Where did that come from? I think that it came from Britain's empire days and their colonial history. People don't always like to reflect back to then or to talk about it but I think it is important because that has become the foundation of how we see 'the other'.

During empire days and during the colonial period, white people were in charge. They possessed everything, they even possessed us. They possessed our fore-parents, our grandparents. Grown men in the community were called 'boy'. Whereas that doesn't happen today in the same stark sense, psychologically and emotionally it still feeds the narrative today, it's underneath.

Me   That's interesting because some people have said to me, 'Slavery and all that is horrible but that's in the past so why can't we just move on as colleagues?'

Rose   We cannot move on until it's been acknowledged. Until those who carry those thoughts acknowledge it. For example, when I came to my appointment here, which was nine years ago, what was it that was really underlying why they didn't want to have me? What was it? Ninety-seven people had applied for the role, why was I shortlisted if on paper I was no good?

Slavery and the enslavement of African people physically damaged us, psychologically and emotionally scarred us. It may not have physically damaged white people but it psychologically and emotionally scarred them and their children and their grandchildren and their great-grandchildren's generation. It is passed down almost as if it's in the DNA.

Me   It's fascinating. I've heard that an apology without action is manipulation.

Rose Yes.

Me   In 2007 there was an apology made for slavery.

Rose I don't even know if there was. Was there really an apology? I don't know whether they made an apology. What I wanted to see was a change.[1]

There was an apology. It said:

THE APOLOGY FOR SLAVERY November 2007

We have listened to one another, we have heard the pain of hurting sisters and brothers, and we have heard God speaking to us.

In a spirit of weakness, humility and vulnerability, we acknowledge that we are only at the start of a journey, but we are agreed that this must not prevent us speaking and acting at a Kairos moment.

Therefore, we acknowledge our share in and benefit from our nation's participation in the transatlantic slave trade.

We acknowledge that we speak as those who have shared in and suffered from the legacy of slavery and its appalling consequences for God's world.

We offer our apology to God and to our brothers and sisters for all that has created and still perpetuates the hurt which originated from the horror of slavery.

We repent of the hurt we have caused, the divisions we have created, our reluctance to face up to the sin of the past, our unwillingness to listen to the pain of our black sisters and brothers, and our silence in the face of racism and injustice today.

But to give Rose her credit, this apology was not from the Church of England. It was from the British Baptist Union Council.[2]

Me   That's what I was going to say. Have you seen any evidence of that repentance?

Rose   Some parliamentarians get it. I believe Mr Speaker gets it.

Me   What is it about him which has opened him to this way of thinking?

Rose   He realises that it is an injustice to live in a world where some people are 'othered', using the phrase that somebody else I met recently used. And 'othered' in such a way that it is negative and they are not allowed to thrive and flourish.

Me   I wonder from your position, have you seen any evidence of change or openness to change?

Rose   Yes and no. I think this is the honest answer.

Me   So it's the psychology?

Rose   Yes. It was articulated best for me when I first went to Hackney. One of the churchwardens said, 'I'm not accustomed to people like you in these positions.' So there's not a policy. There's no procedure. It's just that deep in their psyche, carried over from a legacy of what we were talking about earlier, it is in their psyche that black people are not good enough.

Me   I'm curious, in that case, what biblical or theological models have equipped you or enlightened you as you've navigated your way through?

Rose   We are visible but invisible. And we are invisible because as far as they're concerned we're not meant to be good. We're not meant to be capable, we're not meant to be able. And that's part of the problem. So what has equipped me? Well, I believe very strongly that I am made in God's image.

I believe that I am made in God's image and I believe that I am damn good, as good as any other person who is good. What I have heard myself saying to the church, to the church leadership, is: I refuse to let you repeatedly tell me that I am not good enough ...

When I was a curate up in the Midlands and I was refused doing a funeral or anything like that, I would be very upset but I always have this little inner voice that speaks to me, literally speaks to me, 'Pull yourself together Rose because you do a damn good funeral and it's their loss.' But at first I have to acknowledge the fact that I am hurt. That is painful, the way they have treated me. I don't hide but I never let them see my tears. They won't see my tears.

Me   I'm curious about how to engender that sense of strength across black Anglicans in the UK. Clergy-Laity, within the community because, I guess... I've encountered a couple of things. I've encountered apathy and anxiety when I speak to black colleagues. Even in writing this book, what I've found is people start to tell me their stories but say 'Please don't put it in the book.' There's a reticence, a worry of not wanting to be exposed in a way.

Also what I've found is when I've been in a number of gatherings of black clergy where there's been a white official there, they will speak one way with the white person present... As soon as that person leaves, the real stories come out.

Rose   Yes. Which is nonsense.

Me   Why do you think that is and how can we unlock that and give some sense of confidence to people?

Rose   It is because I think that there is a sense of... What's the word I'm looking for? If we're not in charge then there is a fear that MASSA ('master') will disapprove and punish us. I'm a grown woman now. I'm not playing those games. I'm a grandmother. I respect myself and I want my children to respect me.

I personally have no fear of the church disapproving

of me. One of the things that I'm repeatedly told is that I'm too forthright. I am told this by white people and interestingly I'm told this by black people. Black colleagues who think that I am rocking the boat so I shouldn't be so forthright ... If toning it down means be quiet, I will not be quiet. I will not be silent. I will speak as I see it. I think that I have a responsibility to speak as I see it and I'm not afraid. I'm not afraid because I'm not after any position in the church. All I want to do is serve Christ.

('For women raised to fear, too often anger threatens annihilation. In the male construct of brute force, we were taught that our lives depended upon the goodwill of patriarchal power. The anger of others was to be avoided at all costs because there was nothing to be learned from it but pain ... if we accept our powerlessness then of course any anger can destroy us.')[3]

If the church were to turn round to me and say, 'Sorry, we don't want you to serve,' then I would do what I've always done. I would find it painful but then I would pull myself together and say, 'Rose, it's their loss.'

That is why I have always overstretched myself. I will go for months and months without a day off. I am aware that I overstretch myself but it doesn't bother me because it's for a good cause. I'll go all over the country to speak, which means that I'm up during the night doing my preparation because that's the only time that I have to do it or early morning as well. I'll go to schools because I want them to see that there are other faces in the Church of England.

I've seen the response and the reaction that I have received when I have gone to schools all over the country: the positive reaction that I get from the lay-people, from children, from young people.

Me   I was talking to Elizabeth Henry about this. If the call had been 'We want more black clergy, not for Synod necessarily, but to lift their voices within society at large,' then that would be more appealing to me in terms of media interaction, or speaking on something topical for example.

Rose   It's about how we work within the framework that exists because we're not in a position yet. If we had the resources and we had the numbers then we could say 'Actually no, we need to do this.'

(I think this is the point I struggle with the most within the framework that currently exists. It reminds me of the discussions around CBAC/CMEAC working in the structures. I agree we are a very small constituency, but I believe if we partner across our communities, and across the oceans, we could have numbers and resources to play to our strengths, instead of playing to someone else's tune. But Rose has her own tune and her own drum-kit.)

Me   I'm not sure. When I look at America or South Africa, it feels like there's a greater freedom for them to speak out about issues that pertain to people of colour.

Rose   Yes. They're living it.

Me   When I look at the American system, the clergy network seems more independent. As it developed it leant more towards a Malcolm X philosophy than a Martin Luther King one. It feels there was a more radical punch to it.

Rose   There it is more radical, there is more engagement. But here, there is this fear. I don't know whether it would be unkind to say people are wanting to please. I don't want to please anybody.

Me   Are there any particular biblical characters you resonate with?

Rose   Mary Magdalene is seen as an outcast. People ask: 'What are you doing washing his feet? What are you doing touching the Lord? How dare you touch the Lord. How dare you be so intimate with the Lord!' I feel a little bit of that sometimes. The *Daily Mail* had written that article when I came to this appointment.

Whereas my colleague who got the other half of the role, the headline for him was, 'The Oxford Graduate'. And my headline was, 'The Girl from Montego Bay'. Wow! The Girl from Montego Bay?

But I will turn that around and one day when I write my autobiography it's going to be called 'The Girl from Montego Bay'. You remember that Labi Siffre song? It talks about being good enough.

Me   'Something Inside So Strong'?

Rose   Something inside so strong. That is my song. [She starts singing] 'When they say you're not good enough, just look them in the eye and say I'm going to do it anyway.' Yes.

Me   I'm wondering ...

Rose   *(She forgets I'm there and keeps going)* 'The higher you build your barrier, the taller I become.'

Me   Yes, that's right.

Rose   I'm stronger.

Me   *(I give in and join in too)* 'The further you take my rights away, the faster I will run.'

Rose   *(Her reverie disturbed, she stops singing)* Did you hear my *Desert Island Discs*?

Me   No, I haven't, no.

Rose   I asked for that particular song. I think of the people who try to put stumbling blocks into my way. The people who try to tell me that I'm not good enough or I can't do something. That's my song. That's my theme motif.

In this interview we jumped about looking at South Africa, and America too. What might the relevance be of taking in a larger perspective? May I introduce you to ...

The Whiteness Elephant

When I have shared the concept of my book with white friends, typical responses are: 'There is no racism here in England, is there?' or 'I can't believe there is any racism in the church.' This is often followed up with: 'Places like South Africa during apartheid – now that's what racism looks like, or in America with Black Lives Matter or during the civil rights era, now that is racism. This is a free and fair society.' I have then sought to share something of the covert and subtle forms of racial prejudice I or friends and family have encountered. My white friends have on the whole seemed underwhelmed. The English version of racism has seemed a bit boring, less sensational, less newsworthy, unlikely to lead to a Hollywood blockbuster for the survivors.

It is often more about subtraction of support than addition of suffering; more about a retreat from people of colour than a full-on direct assault. We can all point to the tough-talking skinheads in military fatigues following the British extremist right, with a tattoo of Tommy Robinson on one arm and Katie Hopkins on the other. Considering that form of eruptive and disruptive racism distracts and detracts from the stealthy, banal and mundane forms of racism that are ubiquitous. These forms are the wallpaper of the lives of people of colour into which we cannot blend. It is the toxic air breathed by people of colour, the microscopic particles that are hidden but deadly, eroding the host from the inside out until they are just a shell. I see racism as a single entity that is experienced contextually. It is one and the same animal and that animal is an elephant. Now I am a fan of elephants, so hear this as a metaphor.

The context is different but the creature beneath the surface has the same modus operandi. Do you remember the ancient story of the blind scholars and the elephant? It arises from the Indian subcontinent and may even predate Buddhism. It goes along the following lines: Six blind scholars encounter an elephant but they interact with different parts of the creature's body. They describe the part they touch and touch it as if it were the whole of the elephant because that is the limit of their experience. So one who holds the elephant's leg declares an elephant is like a tree, one who touches the flank declares the elephant is like a wall and so on. I want to update that metaphor and suggest the following.

Black and brown Americans lie beneath the whiteness elephant and say 'Racism is a solid ceiling and is everywhere, and when it wants to it can crush our hope and our lives.' Black and brown people in Britain may feel the sudden slap as the swishing tail leaves a mark, and then they may suffocate with the elephant's toxic bodily fumes, saying 'Racism whips your face when you're not expecting it, and has an invisible stench.' Whereas someone from South Africa might say 'No, racism is sharp, with tusks to impale you.' Someone in the West Indies may describe the trunk, saying that 'Racism is a python that coils around you and slowly suffocates you and imprisons you.'

But it's the same darn White Elephant!

If in the UK racism is usually so nuanced that a number of my white friends are racism atheists, or agnostics, how can their eyes be opened? I think part of the answer is by encountering racism from a different perspective. By an expression of solidarity with those going through racism, and racism going through them, you get the whiff of it, and the Whiteness Elephant can no longer hide in plain sight. In the coming chapter I want to reveal the Whiteness Elephant over the last 50 years in the UK and in General Synod in particular. It is much more about subtraction of support than addition of suffering, but it amounts to the same experience for people of colour. They are on their own.

Notes

1 There was an apology of sorts in 2006, when it was decided in Synod to mark the abolition of the transatlantic slave trade in 2007. Rowan Williams steered the debate towards the church apologising for the part it played in the trade, and the benefits it received when the government compensated slave owners. However, the apology was mixed in that it was also a celebration of William Wilberforce and John

Newton. Having the white heroes present provided a lifeline that those in Synod could grab to prevent the full descent into the watery horror of the transatlantic slave trade. But that water was the water of baptism. There was not a full death moment, so therefore no real resurrection. Just soggy mitres.

2 *Baptists Together* magazine, Spring 2018, p. 7.

3 Lorde, Audre (2018), *The Master's Tools Will Never Dismantle the Master's House*, London: Penguin Classics, p. 32.

5

Get Out of My House!

Up until 1965 those from the Caribbean continued to arrive in England. Most were churchgoers. In some places as many as 69 per cent regularly attended church back on their home Islands.[1] The question hung in the air about whether integration into the established white church would be possible. Sadly, the answer was too often, no.[2] Hill documents that in London 94 per cent of those who had gone to church on their home Islands stopped their attendance.[3] Wilkinson speaks of the pain felt by many at the rejection 'by the mother country and how deeply that rejection had injured the self-understanding of a people'.[4] Wilkinson retreats further into history, relaying the first transgression and tracing the deeper wounds. These are historical scars. He speaks of African-Caribbeans as:

> Recent offspring of a forced liaison between Europe and Africa ... As always in such abuse, hurt reaches deep into the consciousness of all concerned, and can be repressed or ignored only at the cost of personal wholeness and authenticity.[5]

Now, we may relegate these ideas to recent history and think 'Dear, dear, how horrible. Well, let's move on now.' Here is the problem: within the black communities the stories of the abject rejection went viral not just on these shores, but back in the home Islands. The church was exposed as being as racist as other institutions, but didn't acknowledge it. This is the church's original sin. Is there any redemption? The church may claim to want more black and brown recruits, but the message within the black and brown communities is that these are not safe or welcome spaces. For the wellbeing of their own, black and brown families are unwilling to release their children to take fresh-out-of-the-oven cakes and embark on a journey through the woods. They do not want their black and brown children with their red hoodies on to go and visit Grandma. Because we all know that Grandma is not Grandma, she is one of Jadis' pets. She has big eyes, and big teeth, and will devour the child as well as the basket of warm cakes before Little Red Riding Hood can even scream.

The Revd Andrew Moughtin-Mumby has called for lament, a celebration of those who remain faithful to the Church of England despite what they have faced, and a resolve to 'stamp out all forms of racism'.[6] We now turn to versions of those stories Revd Andrew is hoping to highlight.

What was your family's impression of the Church of England? How was it understood by them?

Not positive given that my grandparents were asked to worship elsewhere as their presence was upsetting the congregation in the early 1950s. This was after just one visit at three different churches. This led them to believe that the Church of England didn't want them, which came as a huge shock as they were Anglicans.

Initially my family's impression of the C of E was very negative. The reason being that they felt the C of E had much to do with the enslavement of African people and therefore they did not feel welcomed into the C of E.

A bit dry and boring, white middle-class, middle England, parsons and cricket pitches.

Born and brought up as an Anglican in India so Church of England is the mother-church.

Pessimism. Cautious. Guarded.

The White or English church. Not filled with real prayer from the heart, just traditional, ceremonious or notional words/ worship.

The church that encourages growth of the faith you have come to know (immediate family). The church that is dysfunctional and inhibits growth of the faith you have come to know (wider family).

Growing up in the Caribbean, my family had some familiarity with the Church of England. However, some of them did not have positive notions of the C of E. Some had the idea of it being a 'white man's religion', and it had a cold nature towards black people, and they weren't welcome.

As a compromising church that desperately wanted to fit into society, at the cost of contaminating key Christian principles and doctrines. Highly academic, not very spirit-led and having an elitist nature that looked down on other denominations. Also, historical memories of Windrush generation being told to leave the church.

The people I spoke with described the cautions and perspectives that their families offered to the idea of them joining and getting involved with the Church of England. They had significant hurdles to overcome just to countenance the prospect of joining the church at all. Maybe their families were right to caution them. The following quote chills me. After a disastrous occurrence, black bishop Wilfred Wood felt enough was enough.

Wilfred almost called for a complete secession of black Anglicans from the Church of England.[7]

Three months after the MV *Christena* sank on 4 November 1970, General Synod began with a Communion service at Westminster Abbey. Ahead of this moment the Church of England had had to rely heavily upon parliament to manage its affairs. Archbishop Michael Ramsey and Her Majesty Queen

Elizabeth II both inaugurated the first General Synod. The Rt Revd Colin Buchanan makes the point that during this incredible event, the archbishop and the queen were

> doing a measured pas de deux around each other on the platform, not leaving it entirely clear ... which was host and which was guest.[8]

The devolution of powers to General Synod has been significant. Parliament released General Synod to run many of its own affairs. There is a process whereby General Synod rises from its subservient position to more of a partnership. A freedom and trust is offered, enshrined in law. But this freedom is not passed on. This chapter charts some of the most painful episodes in the life of General Synod with regard to black and brown clergy. We black and brown people of colour in the Church of England have not recovered from this, and white members of the Church of England may not realise but they have also been the casualties of these events; and, being the national church, the nation and beyond has suffered. In 2017 the Cabinet Office produced the Race Disparity Audit[9] which reveals that proportionately more black people volunteer than any other demographic, yet feel the least welcome and secure in their neighbourhoods. In education, housing, immigration, the Windrush scandal; on virtually every scale, black people of African descent are at the bottom. It need not have been so: what if the church had played its part when given the opportunity to demonstrate that it hears and heals?

We have lost three decades of church-based investment into those at the rough end of racial injustice in the poorest and most vulnerable communities. If those in power in the church had had the courage and compassion needed, would we have seen the kinds of headlines which are becoming commonplace in our larger cities? Thirty years ago, the Church of England turned its back on the small fires, and are now complicit in this horrible inferno in which we find ourselves. There is a desire for black labour, but our lives matter less within the Church of England, and our white leadership is woefully ignorant, or deeply reluctant to work within communities tackling racial inequality and to work for racial justice and harmony. While this may be protested, the record within General Synod demonstrates ambivalence at best, and abusive behaviour needing redress at worst.

The Church of England can point to problems in the wider society and rightly advocate for the suffering while at the same time suppressing its own. This is the Cross and the Crown acting against one another.

The Cross and the Crown (Club) has on a number of occasions appeared to take these matters seriously, but in reality has not done so. The Club is the governing body of the Church of England. To the outsider there are a bewildering range of committees. The Archbishop of Canterbury eventually had a council, I guess as his (one day 'her') round-table of various department heads and lead advisors. It is the shipyard where materials are developed that bishop captains can take up to build vessels to take into their dioceses, or dire-seas. Is it about the Cross or is it about the Crown? The way of the Cross is a willingness to suffer alongside the vulnerable, 'a solidarity in diversity', which is one of the phrases of the Bishop of Manchester. When the church prefers status, superiority and security, that is the way of the Crown. But it is always a Club, so by default it skews towards the Crown.

As the Revd Wilfred Wood described the Club, Church of England members saw Christianity as

> the religious expression of their English identity rather than the local manifestation of a universal faith.[10]

It was 1976 and the Race Relations Act of 1965 had been updated with the formation of the Commission for Racial Equality. In July 1977, the Cross and the Crown (Club) debated how to respond, especially as the new Black Majority churches were beginning to rise and beginning to roar, attracting disgruntled and disaffected black Anglicans. With people like Wilfred Wood around it is no surprise that the following was proposed: a Special Church of England Fund to 'finance educational self-help and community projects among Black and Asian communities'.[11]

This step would have been a huge boost, demonstrating that the Church of England was of the Cross and believed that communities with people of colour mattered. Imagine congregations in partnership with those in their wider community. Imagine theological colleges assessing and accessing contextual learning and serving within this interconnecting dynamic of communities. Training clergy from colleges would be learning within the heart of communities, giving those clergy access to broader and deeper human engagement. This would be nothing short of a transformation and an opportunity to be involved in *Trading Places*. But Synod is not the Cross and the Crown alone, it is the Cross and the Crown (Club). There is a membership list, and only certain people are on that list. So even after this Special Fund had been voted for, a fund which could have been understood as a form of rightful reparation, the Board for Social Responsibility (the Church of England department with a remit for community flourishing) simply commended those communities made up of black and brown people, and applied to the existing Projects Fund of the Community and Race Relations Unit of the British Council of Churches.[12] So instead of the Church of England carrying out its Synod-sanctioned duty, it rolled back its commitment.

This said in no uncertain terms: 'This is not our problem' (for 'our' read 'Club'). It said 'We do not need access to education, our housing is fine, we have our pick of careers, we have access to family money, our circles insulate us and ours from the harsher realities others may have to face.' It said 'I'm all right Jackie!' Reparations were not granted, disappointment lingered.

A few years later, Archbishops Robert Runcie and John Habgood, along with the government, set up a commission, a report, into the issues found in urban priority areas, with a desire to get solid recommendations on how to tackle the challenges discovered. The team was assembled, including Wilfred Wood, to really get below the surface and dig deep to figure out how to uproot the problems. In 1985 a thoroughgoing report called *The*

Faith in the City report (FITC) was produced. It held the church and government to account for issues of justice and fairness in society.[13] Four of the 18 members of the commission were from minority ethnic backgrounds – black and Asian – and they were all top thinkers in their various fields.[14] One of the recommendations of the report was to launch a Commission for Black Anglican Concerns. This would have been groundbreaking, the concerns and needs of black and brown communities penetrating communities, empowered by the church, reformatting our colleges, our training, our theology, our teams, and therefore transforming our congregations. Anglican Christians would have been invited and inducted into a deeper, vital, vibrant universal faith as the various rivers and tributaries clashed, crashed and collapsed into one huge family sea.[15]

The later *Called to Act Justly* report said:

all white people are beneficiaries of institutional racism, whether we are aware of it or not. We benefit from it, but it corrupts us. It remains a poison, even if it offers pleasing hallucinatory effects. Ultimately, everyone suffers from racism. Racism is then a social sin that undermines our joint humanity. Our inability to deal with this sin, even if we feel we are not racist in ourselves, is a sin. Our silence is our sin.[16]

The report goes on to say:

for example in dealing with racism, the church needs to acknowledge its structural position within the society in which it finds itself. Thus Sheppard (1983, p. 97) argued that the Church and the world stand together in the face of sin and death, which manifests itself in racial hatred. The Church does not stand by the world, as though impervious to the power of death; it knows that it too has fallen victim to hatred, that it has allowed itself to be torn, shattered, rendered impotent and controlled by racism. Racism is our problem, within our own hearts and minds, and within the Church. Many of the assumptions we make about the other are conditioned by our own cultural experience.[17]

I personify the recommendation to create a Commission for Black Anglican Concerns by conjuring up the iconic image of a West Indian man wearing a trench coat, a fedora hat, jauntily tipped to the side, and holding a suitcase as if he is just off the boat. I am using this character to represent the definition of black as 'the other', outside the scope of the advantages of whiteness. This *Faith in the City* recommendation would finally demonstrate that this character, representing us and all 'others', was accepted home, into the family to which he was returning. One of my respondents called the Church of England 'the mother-church'. This is a common feeling. There is a sense of nostalgia and hope. Wilfred Wood had pointed out that for the West Indian, coming to England was like someone moving from one part of England to another.[18] Much like moving from Bristol to Newcastle, it was the same country with fellow-country folk, it was just that the weather declined, but the warmth of kinship would continue. The report recommended that three posts be created and funded by the Church of England. One post was part of what is known as the Board of Social Responsibility. The BSR's function was to improve communities. The brief of the proposed post was to enable the church to deal with immigration, housing, the unfairness in the justice system, and education. This aspect of the BSR was called the Race and Community Relations Committee, which at that point was led by the Christian Socialist Kenneth Leech. One would think that after the failure to take this seriously in 1977 we would be full steam ahead by this stage. Another post was suggested, intended to help the church recognise that as well as holding up a mirror to communities, the church needed to do the same for itself. It had to get its own house in order, and so recommended that the Church of England employed someone to look at the Cross and Crown (Club) itself. Finally there should be someone to get involved with the colleges. This would flow out of a Standing Commission on Black Anglican Concerns (CBAC).[19] The *Faith in the City* report described how these bodies were all necessary, and would act in tandem.

The *Faith in the City* report made no less than 61 recommendations, including setting up the needed and attractive proposition of the Church Urban Fund. The Cross and the Crown (Club) uses a Standing Committee to help distil and filter its flow of information on behalf of Synod. The Standing Committee was all white. They were all (Club) members. Imagine them as heavyset East End London gangsters playing bouncers. Think of the infamous Kray twins. Let's call them the Ronnie and Reggie Standing Committee. Now see these Lords of the Underworld standing outside a nightclub called General Synod. Ronnie and Reggie are the ones who decide what and who gets in, and what and who does not. Ronnie and Reggie open the doors, unhook the twisted red cord from the rope barrier, and begin to let the guests in. The report's recommendations are the guests traipsing happily into the Club. Once inside, the guests shake hands with the hosts, the Cross and the Crown (Club). The hosts shake hands with 59 of the recommendations from the *Faith in the City* report. Then horns beep, the crowd whoops, and a stretch limo pulls up. Long slender legs swivel out of the limo, followed by a tall, confident, subtly made-up Church Urban Fund. The excitement rushes like a current through the bystanders and waiting recommendations. The Church Urban Fund emerges, a heavy purse slung over her shoulder, purse strings untied, coins dancing out of her purse to the ground below. Her heels clip across the pavement as she joins the end of the queue. She is number 60 in line. Once the Church Urban Fund gets through, Ronnie and Reggie take her in. Once inside, she joins the line to receive her welcome. Then Ronnie and Reggie Standing Committee reapply the rope barrier. They pull the heavy club doors closed. The paparazzi are ushered away and the street becomes quiet. But guess who they leave outside?

In a letter to fellow bishop Colin Buchanan, Wilfred Wood wrote:

> Standing Committee ... decided to recommend 60 of them for acceptance by General Synod. The lone exception was ... a Commission for Black Anglican Concerns ... when the matter [i.e the omission] was debated in Synod, there was much consternation that, although Synod had accepted the

Standing Committees recommendations, Standing Committee was asked to look at the matter again.[20]

The Ronnie and Reggie Standing Committee, these heavyset bouncers, had let 60 guests through the barrier and General Synod had welcomed all but one. This was taken up with the Club management. Wilfred Wood goes on to to describe how key senior church leaders held an emergency meeting and he was tasked with going to meet Ronnie and Reggie Standing Committee. He was fearless, and writes:

> I told them I was not there to accept on behalf of the black community any crumbs that they had to offer. I just wanted to see the faces of a group of people who could be so insensitive ... here was a group, without a single black person on it, who knew better what was good for the black community.[21]

The Cross and the Crown (Club)'s Standing Committee, Ronnie and Reggie, were confronted by their rejected guest now having somehow got in and standing in full view of the Synod chamber, fedora tipped at an angle, conspicuous but composed. The Ronnie and Reggie Standing Committee were not best pleased to have to deal with this ignored recommendation standing before them like a silent sheep before its shearers. The Cross and the Crown (Club) decided the task of taking this further was not to enlist the experts within the *Faith in the City* team, or to draw on the vast amount of data and paperwork that made up the FITC report. Maybe they could have sought out the newly established Commission for Racial Equality for advice, or even the British Council of Churches, who were becoming useful in this field. But no, the management approach is always a 'let's keep it in the family' approach. As this unwelcome guest (let's call him Mr Commission) stands before the Ronnie and Reggie Standing Committee, the Cross and the Crown (Club) management ask Ronnie and Reggie to handle it. Away from the media glare, this was now an in-house issue. It was felt that Mr Commission would upset the cause of church unity. Canon Clarence Hendrickse, a priest born and raised in South Africa, documented the Standing Committee rationale:

There was an underlying feeling within the Standing Committee that groups of black people meeting together might become subversive ... the fear in Synod flowed from the idea of groups of black people coming together and having the power to officially criticise the values, attitudes and modus operandi of Boards or Committees.[22]

As for a commission, here is my definition:

Commission
A group with the authority, agency, and resource granted by a body to act impartially and independently for the good of the whole organisation. Typically a commission is placed alongside the organisation to monitor, investigate, and take appropriate action if deemed necessary.

The reason for this 'commission' was to create an internal measurement tool to eradicate the racism ossifying the bones and marrow of the institution. The 'commission' was to reverse this process, creating greater fluidity in the joints, aiding movement and flexibility. This would have been a good barometer for the work within communities as the congregations could have led the way. We could have seen parallel bodies within the church with a common purpose – to battle racism in communities, battle racism in the colleges and congregations, and in particular battle racism in the Cross and Crown (Club). But that's what Ronnie and Reggie Standing Committee did not want. They thought it went against church 'unity' (I say 'uniformity'). It pushed against the status quo (which is what it was designed to do). After the omission there was a valiant attempt to reinstate the *Commission* on Black Anglican Concerns by the Revd Ivor Smith-Cameron, an Indian priest, in his amendment:

(This Synod) asks the Standing Committee ... to bring forward fully worked out proposals for the establishing of a

Commission of Black Anglican Concerns as suggested ... in *Faith in the City*.[23]

It was backed by the outspoken Bishop of Birmingham and academic, Hugh Montefiore, but a speech against from the Standing Committee, the only speech against, was from Ronnie and Reggie, and the Management supported them. Ronnie and Reggie Standing Committee were afraid that this 'stranger' was going to mess up the Club. But here he was, large as life and twice as real, silently staring everyone down. Enough is enough. Ronnie and Reggie Standing Committee take off their gloves, grab Mr Commission and bundle him out of the room, applying their knuckle-dusters, as everyone but the black and brown members look away. Grunts and groans can be heard from a corridor as business continues. There is a roar of the Club outside but no one recognises it as Aslan any more. Aslan sounds in pain, and his whines and Mr Commission's whimpers merge into an awful dirge. There is a scream, and the noise of a gunshot, then a menacing silence. Business stops momentarily, a door out the back opens and there is the sound of a heavy object being dragged across the floor, followed by the door slamming shut. Moments later the door is opened and the scuffle picks up again, but there is no lion's roar to be heard.

In as much as you did it unto the least of these you did it unto me.

Ronnie and Reggie Standing Committee finish roughing up the 'stranger' in the corridor. A man is brought in, limping yet dignified, wearing the same clothes as the previous man, bloodied and bruised; swollen welts and life-altering facial lacerations make him a ghastly sight. Without close inspection the alteration would not have been clear. After much debate and disappointment from the black and brown members, instead of receiving 'Mr Commission' with power to act, the hero they were given was called 'Mr Committee'.[24]

> **Committee**
>
> A group with delegated powers from a main body or institution authorised to explore a topic in more depth and with a greater level of focus. This is in order to provide comprehensive thinking on a topic which the main body or institution has not the capacity to explore to a similar extent. Committees usually produce reports and are supplemental and subordinate to the main body or assembly.

Ivor Smith-Cameron, who'd moved the amendment, spoke of 'a wave of bewilderment, distress, frustration, and horror through black constituencies both in the Church and in society outside the Church'.[25]

The committee was begun in 1987 – a Committee for Black Anglican Concerns, and Wilfred Wood became its chair. But what was he chair *of* exactly? Mr Committee had no power. He had been dragged off the street, given clothes to wear and beaten to a pulp. Mr Commission could have made an impact. It is like a skilled horse rider seeing her sleek, majestic stallion galloping around the paddock, only to be tapped on the shoulder and looking back to see a braying, bucking donkey, saddled up and ready for her to ride. She mournfully turns to look at the paddock, but the dust is settling, and the stallion is no longer there.

I have some family friends whose teenage son ran away after they mistreated him. As a child I knew him and played with him. He was a little older than me and he felt like a big brother. That was decades ago. Now when I visit these friends there is no record of my childhood playmate. No photo on the walls. He is never spoken about. I never ask and we maintain this illusion that he never existed. Yet his absence screams out, and I often wonder how the family might have looked if he had been cared for and loved, and if they had all had the help they needed to create clear boundaries and a safe environment. In *Reimagining Britain* (to which we will return in the next chapter), Justin Welby speaks of abuse in the family coming from other family members, and their silence and complicit actions. A 'let's keep it in the family' approach. He recognises the reluctance to speak out for fear of suffering more. Well, 'I too am C of E', and I declare that black and brown people have been abused by their mother-church, and their father has given them a stone instead of bread. It is not just Britain that needs to be 'Reimagined' but the idea of church. The Cross and the Crown (Club) needs to be addressed, and redress needs to be made. Justin's analogy works for this situation.

So now we had a committee that was meant to stimulate the reform of the Cross and the Crown (Club). We had no one at all appointed specifically to do the work in our theological colleges. In fact, from 1987, it took until October 2016 for this to happen. It was almost 30 years before that part of the *Faith in the City* report was actioned.[26] We have lost all that time in what could have been incredible, practical and useful training for all clergy to be able to minister to all people.

Back in 1987, Wilfred Wood eventually began to lead the charge when he joined the House of Bishops. Around that time the legend that is Glynne Gordon-Carter, who had arrived from the West Indies, was appointed to do the work of two people. Instead of communities (under the Board of Social Responsibility) having a permanent full-time person and the new committee to combat racism in the Cross and Crown (Club) also having a full-time person, Glynne was expected to cover both briefs. Neither agenda – combating societal racism or tackling institutional racism – was being adequately met, not for lack of enthusiasm or competence but because of the sheer volume of work and expectations. Instead of three people with administrative support, there was one person attempting to carry out two mammoth tasks. Then another death blow was dealt. A bishop decided that Glynne Gordon-Carter should focus more on the 'committee' looking at the Cross and the Crown (Club) and took her away from her role in communities. We went from a desire in *Faith in the City* for a full-time person to inspire the church's stance on societal racism, to a Standing Committee that approved a half-time person trying to hold to this agenda, which a bishop then took away. The radical priest Kenneth Leech was upset. He'd worked hard to get this on the church's agenda and felt betrayed. The chair of the subcommittee on combating race in society quit the group, seeing that without even minimal resourcing it would collapse. It limped on for a while, before reaching its demise. I do not know if the bishop's decision was calculated. I think it was just not comprehensive, and reflected his own concerns, not the concerns of the whole church.

The bishop said 'racism is no longer on the social agenda', but the communities' work needed doing. So now CBAC's role was strangely doubled: fix the Cross and the Crown (Club) and fix our communities, and influence our colleges if you can. Take more responsibility to fix a problem we caused, and do it with fewer resources.

The bucking, braying, donkey, with Wilfred Wood on top, sought to force change on the Cross and the Crown (Club) by getting more black and brown people past Ronnie and Reggie. By now it was 1990. At that time, there were only six black members of Synod, which had around 600 people in it. Synod has a range of committees, and the Committee for Black Anglican Concerns launched a campaign to have 24 extra members who were black or brown, in order to have at least a couple of people present to represent black and brown concerns, and have coverage across most of the boards.

Synod narrowly voted in favour of this motion. Great jubilation followed, but the vote was so close that at the next session of Synod it was taken again, and Ronnie and Reggie Standing Committee pushed for it to be passed not just by the quantity of votes but in all three houses. It failed. To their credit the House of Bishops and House of Clergy voted yes, but the House of Laity voted against. They love me, they love me not. The Committee for Black Anglican Concerns almost resigned, along with other members of General Synod who wanted to express solidarity. Colin Buchanan reflected upon it saying:

Wilfred very nearly called for a complete secession of Black Anglicans from the Church of England ... The sense of rebuff, the sense that, if not actually racist, the Synod was wholly uncomprehending ... these impressions, however subjective, were appalling ... The analysis that they would always slap down the struggling minority community was all too tempting to believe, and that perception bid fair to create, if not wholesale walk-out, yet enormous suspicion and consequent confrontation.[27]

I find Buchanan's use of 'subjective' and 'perception' telling. He had become a bishop at the same service as Wilfred Wood. They were friends, and yet he questioned the reality of their experiences. The threat level he felt was obviously lower. He further states:

I found this episode difficult to evaluate, I was torn between a longing that Black Anglicans should play a developing – and guaranteed – role in the Synod and yet a contrary sense that the preferred route was grievously misconceived.[28]

He then launches into a rant about women's ordination and about creating an easy way into Synod for 'white people who might have labelled themselves as "black" for an easy (if scandalous) route into Synod'.[29]

So it goes back to protecting the Cross and the Crown (Club) as the overriding principle.

Desmond Tutu

Glynne Gordon-Carter was considering her options. She and others had convinced many people to prepare to stand for General Synod. It was safe now, she had assured them. They should come and get involved. So now she held the pain of their disappointment too. She said:

For me the turnaround came as a result of attending a Celebration in Birmingham at the NEC on Saturday 22 April 1989. Archbishop Desmond Tutu was the specially invited guest. The theme for the day was 'Freedom to the Oppressed'. It was inspiring to hear Archbishop Tutu preach and to meet him after the service. The Archbishop's words to me were ... 'so you are the lady who Bishop Wood tells me is working in the church to combat racism' ... I was thrilled and felt uplifted![30]

What if 'Freedom to the Oppressed' did not mean staying with the oppressor? What if Wilfred Wood had mounted his bucking, braying, donkey and left? The Management at the Cross and the Crown (Club) were getting worried this might happen, and pulled in Ronnie and Reggie Standing Committee for a word. Ronnie and Reggie were told to apologise to the poor black and brown people. The apology said:

The Standing Committee regrets that the failure of the ... measure should have attributed to the severe alienation, hurt and rejection experienced by the many black peoples in relation to the Church of England and affirmed its conviction that there should be fuller participation by black people in Synodical Government at all levels, including the General Synod, its Boards and Councils.[31]

So, a case of 'sorry, not sorry' from old Ronnie and Reggie, because in spite of what was said the (Club) is for members only. But like a runaway teen returning to the home where a violent father is waiting, or a battered wife coming back to an abusive partner, Wilfred turned the donkey around, and Glynne, emboldened by Desmond, walked back into the burning building.

'After a great deal of deliberation, CBAC agreed to continue with its work.'[32] Desmond Tutu's inspiration and the forced apology got the committee back to work. Desmond Tutu's visit had a detrimental effect on Bishop Colin Buchanan too. He was the chair of the multi-ethnic ecumenical church group who had organised his visit. There was racist propaganda aimed at the organisers, calling Desmond Tutu dangerous because of his association with Mandela. The Tory minority in Birmingham

City Council were also set against the visit, and Colin was told that the opposition to the visit meant they had lost a six-figure sum, and that the Diocese of Birmingham would have to pick up the tab. He felt the need to resign and spent a year in what he calls an exile.[33] Desmond Tutu unwittingly exposed a white man who bowed to the establishment and fell on his sword for the Crown. This seems in contrast to someone like Trevor Huddleston or John Collins. Tutu also managed to provide the opposite message to his talk about freedom by inadvertently sending Glynne back into the firing line.

Thankfully she had a bucket and a hose. She had been inspired by a trip to Canada, where 180 Native Canadian Anglicans had gathered to affirm one another in their God-given identity, so that they could find mutual solidarity and set the agenda for the Anglican Church of Canada to follow. A UK version of this celebration of black Anglican identity was set for 1994 and, in what seems to me to be a departure from the Canadian example, in the UK there was an imperative that:

The dates should be acceptable to the Archbishops of Canterbury and York as their attendance would be vital.[34]

Why? Was it because we wanted 'they love me, they love me not' to end on 'they love me'? Gordon-Carter documents:

It was indeed a watershed because for the first time in the life of the Church of England, Archbishops, Bishops and other key people in the church were meeting with black Anglicans to discuss, share, pray, worship, laugh, play and eat together over a weekend residential conference. It was a watershed experience because for the first time black Anglicans were coming together from all over England and from different persuasions to be seen, heard, listened to and affirmed in their ministries as laity and clergy.[35]

There is an assumption of equality of peers meeting and sharing. The bishops stated how gracious the black and brown Anglicans were, one saying:

It was organised with graciousness and without rancour. It was the relaxed style and the good humour of the conference which struck me most.[36]

Really? There is no power analysis here, no thought of how the dominant white worldview was crushing true freedom of speech. The status of the bishops is not assessed or challenged. The conference had conversations describing the challenges of racial injustice and what struck this bishop most was how nice the black and brown people were to him. But perhaps the responsibility is shared. One white bishop with good intentions told the black and brown people what to do, and they listened. He stated:

I urged the Committee to prepare a public statement. There was initial reluctance. 'We don't want to sit up half Saturday night.' I responded unrelentingly 'Here is a once-in-a-decade opportunity to blaze something into the press and into the hearts and minds, and you cannot stay a couple of hours out of your beds to do it?' It happened, a trumpet call to the plenary session.[37]

So what did these sleep-deprived members of a committee who were encouraged – ordered – by a white man in power, come up with late that night? This was their statement:

Black people are people. Black Christians are Christians. Black Anglicans are Anglicans. Our ethnic origins may lie in Asia, Africa or the Americas, and a few of us are visitors from those lands, but mostly we ourselves are English, a large proportion of us born in England, and glad to be Anglicans here in partnership with white Christians. We belong to this land and every corner of it. Make us more visible within the life and leadership of our Church. Racism has no place in Christ; so let all discrimination against us, knowing or ignorant, cease. Let us reach our fullness in Christ as ourselves. Let our gifts and calling be recognised and affirmed, our partnership in the life of the Church of England be evident and welcomed ... Let the whole Church of England by deliberate will live this doctrine in practical love.[38]

Would such a statement have been produced if white people were not the intended audience? There is a continuation of the same project to get into the Cross and the Crown (Club). There is a pleading, but it is a reverse fairytale. Do you know the story of the three little pigs where the wolf threatens to blow the house down? Well, in this statement (which follows on from the failed attempt to increase members of Synod, which follows on from the murder of Mr Commission and the instigation of Mr Committee, which follows on from the community fund being rejected, and so on ...), this is the story of the little pig trying with all her might to break into a house full of Jadis' whiteness wolves. Her hooves red raw from banging, pleading that she is also a wolf, just paler and less hairy, but she deserves to be in the (Club) too. God help her if the key clicks in the lock, the handle is depressed and she is let in.

But one good thing seemed to flow from this conference. The Archbishop of Canterbury (then George Carey), having been exposed to diverse forms of worship, prayer and liturgy, declared in his keynote address:

I believe it is a dimension that will not only enrich our worship and liturgical life but will also add something exciting to our evangelism. I urge you to develop it and if you do, I can promise you my enthusiastic support.[39]

CBAC had changed its name to CMEAC for Committee for Minority Ethnic Anglican Concerns, Bishop John Sentamu was now chair and, again buoyed by 'they love me', they came up with these three aims to respond to the archbishop's words:

1 To explore ways and means of ... bringing together our rich diversity of gifts – music, poetry, art, drama, dance – as an offering to the Church
2 To explore how to release people to glorify God within the structures

3 To explore how to make a contribution to discussion on liturgies in the Church of England, as all liturgies were going to be revised in the year 2000.

This phrase 'within the structures' assumes that the structures were neutral, benevolent, and inherently open. But remember that little pig banging on the door, unaware it is full of wolves. Think of the passenger vessel where the boat is taking on water, behaving erratically, and yet black and brown people are being invited to board. By now we should anticipate what happened next.

George Kovoor, a confident Indian who had become a British citizen in order to fully participate in mission and growing faith, was principal of a missionary training college, Crowther Hall. He was made chair of the sub-liturgical group to seek to meet the above objectives. The chairman of the main Liturgical Commission met with George to be made aware of the work being done. There was a burst of excitement but Glynne Gordon-Carter mournfully recounts:

the lack of staff resources to focus on the area of work, as well as the busy schedules of members, resulted in the work going into abeyance.[40]

George was later principal of Trinity College in Bristol, which is where I trained for ministry, and so we knew one another. At Trinity College, George sought to expose us to a range of worship experiences arising from different cultures, with differing underlying philosophies of life. He did what he could to bring an international flavour to the forms of theological encounter. Until reading about the Liturgical Commission, I did not realise that George was demonstrating at Trinity what could have been church-wide. I contacted him to hear his side of the story of these events. He began by speaking about the richness and the full sensory experience of Indian culture. He spoke about the multiple ways one could encounter God. He said:

The worship in the Church of England is cerebral, it is designed for those who can read and write. Coming from India there is the use of the body, of posture, one prostrates oneself, there is chanting, melody and harmony and repetition of phrases in order to let the words go in deeply and transform you. Worship is encounter with God, worship is not sanctuary bound, it is about living an examined life, times of silence and contemplation.

George also had something important to say on church rubrics. These are the instructions, the rules that govern how one presents the prayers and the readings. They are like director's notes to an actor – where one should stand, when the congregation should sit, which way they should face, which parts of the given service are core and which sections are optional. George was spelling out that the accepted rubrics could be restrictive. For example, he spoke about Bible readings being accessible and dynamic.

This type of liturgical reformation excited me, for several reasons. For one, it was missional. With the huge growth of Eastern philosophy, the boom of yoga, and now mindfulness, imagine if the church had embraced something of this vision. Churches could have been centres of deep community and communal encounter. For another, this was an inclusive vision. I am dyslexic and dyspraxic, so being permitted to paint with more colours, operate with more notes of the scale, truly loving God with mind, emotion and body, or in thought, word and deed, would have been liberating. When I asked George why it did not happen he said:

The mindset was too Anglo-Saxon. There was an old boys' club. I was seen as the token, the exotic one with strange and novel ideas, the minority expression could never be the majority experience. People would say 'Come and look at what George is doing', but it was seen as an interesting one off, never something to be adopted more widely.[41]

But what if it had been? Barry Thorley, who was one of the founders of the Association of Black Clergy, reflects on his time post-retirement at his Congregation's African house at Keur Moussa in Senegal:

> I stayed there a year, probably one of the happiest years of my life. Being welcomed all the way into the choir and to receive communion, I sang their wonderful fusion of Benedictine Plainchant and local Wolof and Mandinka village music, whose modal structures were a miraculous match. We sang to the accompaniment of balafon, tam tam and kora, a stringed harp-like instrument.[42]

What can the white bishops do?

The story of USPG, the United Society for the Propagation of the Gospel, interests me. It has travelled a journey from oppressor of, to acting in solidarity with, others. As SPG, it was involved in the slave trade to varying degrees. It had slaves who had the word 'society' branded on their chests. But over time it developed a conscience and matured its approach. One of the most interesting groups of USPG, I think, were the 'atheists of the empire'. These were white missionaries who spoke up and out against the imperial project and the pain it inflicted on the world. They, like the community organisers of today, empowered the people on the ground to develop grassroots initiatives, nurturing leadership and instilling pride in the home context, thereby offering an alternative lens through which the local people could understand themselves. It is no wonder, then, that this group directly inspired future firebrands like Trevor Huddleston. They changed their name to 'US' (the United Society) to try and shun the past associations, but that did not quite work and eventually they went back to USPG with a new meaning: 'United Society for Partnership in the Gospel'. In time, I would love to hear of groups of radical bishops sabotaging the (Club) and mentoring others to share the kingdom and repudiate the empire.[43]

Notes

1 Hill, C. (1963), *West Indian Migrants and the London Churches* London: Oxford University Press p. 16.

2 Beckford, R. (2000), 'Doing Black Theology in the UKKK', *Black Theology: An International Journal* 4: 38–60, p. 35.

3 Hill, *Migrants*, p. 23.

4 Wilkinson, J. (1993), *Church in Black and White,* Edinburgh: St Andrew's Press, p. 11.

5 Ibid., p. 2.

6 www.churchofengland.org/sites/default/files/2020-01/GS%20 2156A%20Windrush%20Commitment%20and%20Legacy.pdf.

7 Buchanan, Colin (2006), *Taking the Long View*, Church House Publishing, p. vii.

8 Ibid., p. 7.

9 https://assets.publishing.service.gov.uk/government/uploads/ system/uploads/attachment_data/file/686071/Revised_RDA_report_ March_2018.pdf.

10 Udo, D. (2007), *We Shall Overcome*, London: Root and Branch Consultancy, p. 40.

11 Buchanan, *Long View*, p. 141.

12 Ibid.

13 *Faith in the City: A Call for Action by Church and Nation : Report of the Archbishop of Canterbury's Commission on Urban Priority Areas, Church of England*, London: Church House Publishing, 1985.

14 Buchanan, *Long View*, p. 143.

15 Gordon-Carter, G. (2013), *An Amazing Journey*, London: Church House Publishing.

16 *Called to Act Justly: a challenge to include minority ethnic people in the life of the Church of England*. Report by the Stephen Lawrence Follow-Up Staff Group April 2003, London: Church House Publishing, p. 7.

17 Ibid., p. 7.

18 Wood, Wilfred and Downing, John, 1968, *Vicious Circle*, SPCK, London, p. 5.

19 Gordon-Carter, *Journey*, p. 19.

20 Buchanan, *Long View*, p. 144.

21 Ibid.

22 Ibid., p. 19.

23 Ibid., p. 145.

24 Ibid., p. 19.

25 Gordon-Carter, *Journey*, p. 19.

26 www.churchtimes.co.uk/articles/2016/11-november/features/features/are-the-blinkers-still-on.

27 Buchanan, *Long View*, p. 146.

28 Ibid.

29 Ibid.

30 Gordon-Carter, *Journey*, p. 27.

31 Ibid.

32 Ibid.

33 Buchanan, *Long View*, p. 4.

34 Gordon-Carter, *Journey*, p. 57.

35 Ibid., p. 61.

36 Ibid.

37 Buchanan, *Long View*, p. 148.

38 Ibid.

39 Gordon-Carter, *Journey*, p. 67.

40 Ibid., p. 68.

41 The American Episcopal church has been thinking this through and I refer you to www.anglicanmultiethnic.org/looking-at-the-2019-bcp-multi-ethnic-challenges-for-a-missional-church/. This is a great essay pertaining to the Book of Common Prayer.

42 www.st-barnabas.org.uk/wp-content/uploads/2018/10/Chronicle-84-2018.pdf pg 15.

43 www.uspg.org.uk/about/history/.

6

Reimagining *Reimagining Britain*

Our ethnic origin is the first and most obvious example
of the power which kinship and affinity have over us. The
fact of skin colour has made ethnic minorities obvious and
immediate targets for the defensive, discriminatory activities
of dominant ethnic majorities.[1]

These are the words of retired bishop Peter Selby. He attacks
the (Club). Selby considers that one of the main restrictions
on black empowerment and agency is discrimination. He
recognises and highlights the ignorance of confusing 'Christian
civilization with the customs and practices of dominant or
majority groups'.[2] Whatever the motive for oppressive and
ignorant practices, he calls it a form of 'genocide' against
minority cultures.[3]

For 40 years and more black and brown Church of England
members and clergy and a few white allies have been saying that the church is institutionally racist, but their voices
have been minimalised and marginalised. The Revd Andrew
Moughtin-Mumby's private motion in February 2020 for
Synod to apologise for its treatment of the Windrush generation was heard in General Synod. His appeal led to a swift
rejoinder from Archbishop Justin Welby as reported in the
Independent, which said:

Mr Welby, in off-the-cuff remarks given after he said he felt
the need to 'ditch' his prepared speech following the Revd
Moughtin-Mumby's words, told the Synod he was 'almost
beyond words'.

He said: 'Personally, I am sorry and ashamed. I'm ashamed of our history and I'm ashamed of our failure.' He added: 'There is no doubt when we look at our own church that we are still deeply institutionally racist. Let's just be clear about that. I said it to the College of Bishops a couple of years ago and it's true.'[4]

Well, a couple of years before, when the Archbishop of Canterbury told the College of Bishops about institutional racism, his book *Reimagining Britain* was coming out. Let us turn now to the archbishop's more in-depth reflections. I should say that this is Justin's description, as he is careful to state that this book is his own thoughts and not pronouncements of the church.

The views here expressed are my own, not an official position of the Church of England or the Anglican Communion ... no one person or group can definitively decide what the Church thinks.[5]

Nevertheless the thinking, research and writing on these macro topics are coming from the head of the one who wears the mitre, carries the crosier and sits on the throne. Throughout his book there is an expected and welcome plea for strong community. He refers to two different community stories, one from the Hebrew Scriptures and the second from the New Testament. Welby says: 'Community ... speaks to us of the assurance that "we are all in it together".'[6]

There are many great episodes of community in the Bible and numerous stories of seeking to establish it. Two leading examples are the exodus of the people of Israel from Egypt ... and the early years of the New Testament community of the Church ... The impact of both these stories has been monumental.[7]

I am nodding along – the exodus story is foundational. Our heritage, our sense of self, our self-determination is predicated on this story. I love the epic imagination of the authors and editors as they instil into the Jewish cultural memory a story of overcoming insurmountable odds through resistance, resilience and revolution as the emerging nation fought to establish their place in that contested land, annihilating some, assimilating others, as they grew in strength and power. The exodus story documents the power of the collective human spirit to come back from the brink and be remade for a new context.

Then Justin says this:

> In the UK, the exodus story is reduced in impact for *most of us*[8] because – at least at the national level – we have not known slavery, occupation or oppression for a very long time.[9]

I sink in my chair as I realise his book is not written with me in mind. Justin is not picturing me, a black clergyman, as his reader. But before I simply think this book is just for white British people, Justin goes on to clarify that the exodus story

> resonates in Northern Ireland, Scotland, and Wales, and with many minority communities across the UK, whether around ethnicity, disability, gender or sexuality.[10]

He introduces quite an extensive list of those for whom the exodus story has meaning. So, who then is the 'most of us' for whom the exodus story has limited impact? If it is not the Scottish, Welsh, or Northern Irish (Irish?), minority (token) ethnic, those differently abled, women, and those of the LGBTI+ communities, who is he thinking about? By a process of elimination it would appear the 'us' is none other than white, wealthy, able bodied, straight/cis-gendered English males. The movie *Notting Hill* was critiqued for portraying an area devoid of colour and culture other than white, quite at odds with the earthy, full-bodied and technicolour reality. So how narrow is Justin's lens? How determined is his directorial vision, that he casts his movie called 'community' full of people like himself?

Black theologian Robert Beckford argues that the 'White church and European theology has a particular disposition towards cultural racism(s)'.[11] This has an edge, and it is no surprise that it comes in the essay 'Doing Black Theology in the UKKK'. On a deeper reading of the work, Beckford is saying that other ethnic traditions are often disregarded. He highlights this trend when quoting (the then) Bishop Sentamu:

> The organisational culture of the Church of England ... is still socially glued together by a culture that is monochrome – that is White ... it lacks colour and spice.[12]

A member of the Cross and Crown (Club) responded to John Sentamu's comments by saying:

> The Culture of the C of E has its legitimate historic origins as well as a present-day reality in which 'white English culture' should not be apologetic or accused of 'lacking spice'. A cultural dog's dinner is not necessarily superior.[13]

I found the comparison disturbing, that the given alternative to white English culture is a 'cultural dog's dinner'. This cultural hegemony is exercised in a way that overrides other valid starting points. Beckford claims that this expectation impacts theology: 'the theology of Anglicanism supports the maintenance of the White male hierarchy'.[14] Beckford's comments seem too pessimistic until we discover that Justin is not alone in that cohort of priests who draw a ring around the 'us' which excludes the 'them' and has the power to define the 'them' and the power to silence the 'them'.

The Silent Choir

I worked as a youth worker in a large multi-ethnic Church of England parish. I was pleased when the white English vicar gave me an assignment outside my usual remit. There had been some grumbling among a few black women, who were asking to meet the vicar and share their thoughts on how the church could better reflect them. He was uncomfortable with their request and did nothing. In fact he went to great lengths to avoid them. But they persisted and he felt pressured when these women began to share their difficulties with minority ethnic staff to pass on to him. I thought he wanted to change things when he asked me to conduct interviews among the minority ethnic groups to establish how effective the church was in ministering to them. I saw myself as being called to bring peace. I respect, and respected, the vicar. I was convinced I could help him grow and embrace his wider congregation, who came weekly, gave regularly and had as much right to be heard as anyone else.

At this stage the church had around 2,000 people, had a young profile and was perceived as progressive. This felt like a real opportunity to serve the church by unleashing the voices of more of its members. The staff team was quite large and I rounded up several staff members from minority ethnic backgrounds, and they too were excited at the potential of the project. They had received the complaints and we collectively felt this was a real opportunity to do something positive about it in a way which would take everybody with us. Between us we amassed a list of names of contacts that we had – regular church members who were from black and minority ethnic backgrounds. We compiled questionnaires that considered themes of hospitality, welcome, worship, preaching, and the social life of the congregation. Over the next couple of months we met with dozens of people and conducted the interviews. We came back together, amassed our findings and studied the data.

We discovered through the feedback of the participants that the church was not perceived to have an integrated approach to those of minority ethnic backgrounds. In fact, it became apparent that an upper middle class Englishness was the normative expectation of behaviour and mode of engagement. The teaching at the church was seen as irrelevant in addressing the needs and personal challenges of our interviewees' deepest lives. There was an unstated assumption that the majority ethnic group norms, the examples used in the sermons, and the solutions offered in the small groups, would work well for all. The majority ethnic group understood themselves in non-ethnic terms as simply 'charismatic evangelical Christians'. There was not an explicit recognition of them being 'white charismatic English evangelical Christians', and the respondents felt this blindness of the majority ethnic group meant that they were presented with a set of assumed universal truths that were equally applicable to all.

Our little committee was concerned about how the report would go down. The grumblers were told we had this in hand and they could trust us, the process, the vicar, and God to do the right thing. We gave copies to the other clergy, who without question, saw in what we had done a real opportunity for the church to take a huge stride forward and widen its frame of reference to incorporate more people within the picture – to acknowledge the stories and hopes of all its members, not just the members who looked, sounded and dressed like the vicar. I created a number of easy wins, positive engagements that would lift the visibility of minority ethnic groups and create greater exposure.

In my head it was the perfect way in, a colour-neutral approach to warm him up. He could surely appreciate stylistic differences if not substantive differences. Once he had begun to build trusted relationships with black and minority ethnic people, having them in his home, and maybe venturing into some of theirs, he would be more ready for phase two, which would be learning the stories they had that were outside his frame of reference. Then phase three would begin to introduce some complexity, open him up to class differences and see how he could work towards reimagining his church to cater for a wider group. Then, as with this book, I had a number of voices which the rigour of research had transformed into a choir – music with pain, hunger and hope. People were at my back praying for me. My staff colleagues were anticipating a celebration. I left the office to walk to his vicarage document in hand.

After ringing the doorbell, the vicar's wife answered the door and sent me upstairs to his office. I skipped up the flight of stairs and stepped inside, bursting with joy at this new opportunity for the church to evolve and deepen. He often spoke about us being adventurous Christians, and what I held was a map for a great adventure. I tempered my enthusiasm, unsure if his English reserve could accommodate the energy surge I was feeling.

I presented my report to the vicar. I pre-empted my presentation with 'there are challenges, and there are suggestions of how we tackle them'. The positive recommendations included featuring a number of successful black and minority ethnic members at the front of the services, having them share what they do for their jobs, in the arts, and business; also I recommended that he included them within his weekly post-evening-service vicarage soirées, as well as occasional Sunday lunches for those with families.

He perched on his swivel chair, accepted and held my document, which was teeming with comment, conversation, grief and expectation. The voices within the document were clearing their throats ready to sing out powerful possibility and purpose. He looked at me for a moment then spun round in his chair and in a single move dropped it onto the top of his in-tray. He deftly spun back around to meet my gaze. I could feel a coolness in the air as, in his rich baritone voice, he declared: 'The spirit is saying now is not the time for diversity, now it is the time for unity.'

Each word exploded a miniature bomb within me. The heat from the internal blasts fragmented my thinking. The authority and measured tone he used betokened that no response was necessary or expected. He stood first. It took me a half second to read the cue and stand, shake his hand, and conjure a smile as I walked back down the steps. I limped further back into the dungeon I had promised the people we had interviewed we would all be released from. The vibrant voices of the document fell silent. I wondered if, when the vicar left his office, the in-tray rattled with the screams of the unheard voices. This English establishment vicar had pulled the Holy Spirit card. He was claiming God as his source of authority to cancel out the validity and value of the multiple conversations I and my team had conducted. One strong voice infused with privilege, claiming God-like knowledge, killed the promised reform, promoting not unity but uniformity.

There is a tension in being a minority ethnic person with a minority ethnic voice. It is difficult to shift from the minor to the major key. This musical vacillation is captured in David Isiorho's essay referring to racism within the Church of England. He concludes his paper with a sober realisation of the task ahead but has a hopeful note when he calls for

> the Church of England to rediscover its prophetic voice through radical identification with the oppressed. Just as black and Asian Christians have had to wrestle free from colonialism, theological educators will have to reclaim a biblical sense of English identity, reclaiming a whiteness which is non-oppressive and willingly relinquishes the myth of primacy.[15]

But this vision feels a world away from where we are now. Which white theologians make the demolition of white superiority a key feature of their work and practice? How can their voices find wider coverage?

Both Justin and the vicar of the church I worked at seem to indicate that while the 'us' do not know the impact of being slaves, the occupied, or the oppressed, they have forgotten that it was their ancestors who were on the other side of the equation, oppressing, enslaving and doing the occupying. And it is *they* who currently still benefit from historic injustices. However, at least I am seen in some way by Justin, aka Archbishop of Canterbury, head of the Anglican Communion; my struggle is recognised. Even if there appears to be a privileging of his crowd, at least I am seen. I am one of the 'them', but my struggle is real. Except that it is not.

> Among the great and beneficial changes have been radical improvements in the status of groups that were previously oppressed: women, ethnic minorities, those with disabilities, those with varieties of sexual orientation and identity.[16]

By minimising the ongoing oppression for the 'them', and failing to name and delineate the privileged 'us', both the oppressor and the oppressed are rendered invisible.

But where I see he is right in his analysis is that – as he comments in the fuller piece – both devolution in the movement of power away from the centre and human rights protecting the vulnerable have formed a new ideology:

> The development of a deep suspicion of power made government more difficult but served many groups well. The changes were not only in culture ... Status was no longer seen as giving entitlement to power. The move began towards devolution ... more and more centrality to the individual, to autonomous decision-making and to suspicion of ancient rules and institutions. The change has been uncomfortable for many of those institutions, but often powerfully effective for those who in the past were marginalized, and genuinely the victims of power groups.[17]

What I was waiting to read was an acknowledgement, an admission, that the church itself is one of these institutions under suspicion from the 'them', that the 'us' have been involved in an accretion of power, not its distribution. What of the other model of community and church Justin mentions? We've had the exodus model where Justin says: 'where inequality and the abuse of power are great, the exodus spoke of the care of God for the poor and oppressed'.[18]

But we have established that it is no longer relevant to the 'us' because slavery does not apply, and it is not relevant to the 'them' because things are better now. Maybe we should look at the other model, based on the early Christian community known as the early church. In the section on community Justin comments that in this model 'even deepest ethnic differences can be overcome and where people seek to take unfair and deceitful advantage, God steps in powerfully'.[19]

Good – let's look into that association of the early church with power and racial inequality. That is how I am reading this passage. However, throughout the book there is an appeal to economic equality but not racial equality, because in a UK context, racial inequality is already settled in his worldview. We have to wait until a few chapters later to hear Justin's fuller description of the early church in his essay on education. He quotes a section of Acts that shows how everyone was of 'one heart and soul' and also how the apostles shared out to those in need.[20]

He then gives his basis for this community being special. I was wondering how the deep ethnic differences would be overcome. Justin says: 'it is clear there was at least an extraordinary group, since the infant church grew so rapidly'.[21] Remember that the exodus narrative is no longer in play here in his thinking. The framing of 'oppressor' and 'oppressed' is no longer relevant. It is a moot point. The growth of the church in numerical terms is judged to be the mark of a successful and extraordinary group. This is about economics, growth, and 'even the ethnic tensions' are about race relations, horizontal interactions, not racial justice which accounts for the vertical power gap. He goes on: 'Community is formed in sharing and flourishing communities that gather up the weak and the strong, enabling all to benefit from all.'[22] That sounds good. Justin goes on to admit how rare this is. But on a second reading surely the strong are doing better in the distribution of the flourishing, the weak are at the mercy of the strong to share what they have. But as long as the promoted framework is positive horizontal relationships, the other realities remain hidden. The weak and the strong privately keep their other labels of 'oppressed' and the 'oppressor', the victim and the perpetrator. It is superficial race relations over deep racial justice. What about the archbishop before Justin?

I interviewed Tunde Roberts, a Nigerian clergyman with a long history with people of colour in the church, the one-time chair of the Association of Black Clergy who has had a considerable journey with the Church of England. He is a true elder who loves the church enough to work with it in spite of the many obstacles he has had to overcome to simply exercise his God-given vocation.

Me   Before we started recording, you mentioned going to an event with the outgoing archbishop Rowan Williams.

Tunde Years ago in Westminster and the Bishop of London then, Richard Chartres, very kindly invited him to come and speak to us, all the clergy within the diocese, and I was there. And a gentleman asked him a question: 'What have you done regarding minority ethnic people?' and he simply said 'I failed, that is one area I could have done much, much more and I didn't do anything' and so he said that, and I was saying 'This is our story, people who are in a position of authority and they only think about us when they are on their way out, this has been our story.'

Me   Did he give any explanation as to why?

Tunde No, no. I remember when he was made the Archbishop of Canterbury and I was the chair of the Association of Black Clergy, and Archbishop Sentamu was then Bishop of Birmingham, and we held our residential in Birmingham and he was invited to come and speak to us, and one of the things he said was that 'Like yourself, I am not part of the Church of England, my background is the Church of Wales, I am a stranger like yourself', that was how he put it and he continued, 'I will make sure that I stand up for you' and he failed, he didn't do that. On that occasion, on our residential, we pushed him on that, saying: 'Very little has been done regarding minority ethnic people' and he said 'Look, I am one of you, I am coming from the Church of Wales into the Church of England, so I am like you and I will ensure that I will look at issues concerning minority ethnic people', but he never did that.

Me   Do you have any thoughts, or theories or considerations as to what prevented him, or what resistance he had, or what resistance was within him, or hesitations he had either personally or ...

Tunde I don't know, but he spent a lot of time with the issues of the Anglican Communion and that probably overwhelmed him. The issue of the breakaway Lambeth Conference, all these provinces trying to do their own thing and people going their own way. And that took a lot of his time, but actually if he had put minority ethnic people in senior positions, that would have actually helped him, because most of these people are in African provinces, African dioceses, and that could have helped him.

Me   So he had a whole team of ambassadors waiting and he didn't activate them.

I had another conversation with a bishop who remained off the record. He had this to say when comparing Justin with his predecessor:

If you look at the College of Bishops, it was all male at that stage and it was 99 per cent white, and you could probably say it was also almost 100 per cent over-55s, and I actually think what the present Archbishop of Canterbury has done is very significant. Now you might say it's still working in margins, but you look at the number of women who are now in the College of Bishops, and although it is still pitifully small, we are beginning to see some BAME people consecrated as bishops and I think history will look back and say one of Justin's greatest legacies to the Church of England is that he has driven this through. He has not been willing to stand and say that was good enough, because it wasn't, and our previous archbishop, Rowan, found it hard to drive change through in this way.

Could the reason Rowan failed, and was not able to drive through change, be because of his self-acknowledged outsider status? Was he tasting a little of the black experience within the system? Are the levers of power better designed for a Justin Welby-like character? Let's take another look at Archbishop Rowan's record.

Reimagining Lambeth

There are three instruments of communion overseen by a fourth; the Archbishop of Canterbury. The Archbishop of Canterbury chairs the meeting of the Primates of those 39 provinces in communion with the See of Canterbury. He is also the president of the Anglican Consultative Council, and he calls the Lambeth Conference every ten years. The Lambeth Conference is the biggest ship in which, every ten years, we Anglicans from around the world set sail.

Archbishop Ndungane represented the oldest African Anglican province of South Africa. He was a man who wanted to effect change. He had issued the invitation for the Lambeth Conference to be relocated for the first time since it began in 1867. On 28 June 2004, the Lambeth Conference Design Committee released a missive that stabbed at the heart of the 'two-thirds Anglican' world, reopening a wound that would take another two decades to be repaired. The message bore the news that the emerging plan for a Lambeth Conference in South Africa had been cancelled due to lack of support.

This would have been a deep uprooting of the conference from English soil. No tea in the gardens of Buckingham Palace, no boat ride on the Thames. Ndungane desired that the conference should be held in Cape Town. The desire to relocate one of the highest bodies of the Anglican Communion was that of rewriting the paradigm of host and guest, or of parent and child. Replanting the Lambeth Conference on African soil could have liberated the conference and enriched it within another soil and environment to help catalyse dormant shoots. The Archbishop of South Africa, Ndungane, questioned why the conference of the Primates should always be hosted in England. In fact he went as far as to say: 'Is it morally defensible, for instance, in a diverse, global context that representatives of our family should return to the perceived "motherland" for the conference?'[23] He queried why, if the archbishop is first among equals, the others could not take a turn at hosting. Archbishop Rowan Williams was positive about the idea, saying: 'New times require a new kind of Lambeth conference.'[24]

However, despite the positive reception in principle, the money did not follow. The $10,000,000 price tag of the conference, as it was expected to be run, could not be raised. The design team had done all they could to raise the money through individuals and institutions but there was not the confidence of the investors to back the idea. This was partly because the conference was contested for other reasons.[25] The American Episcopal Church had consecrated Gene Robinson as bishop. Gene Robinson was in an openly gay relationship, which contradicts the current stance of the Church of England. Each province around the globe is at liberty to set their own rules and guidelines; however, everyone had a view on this. An earthquake resulted from this fault-line, leaving the American church split on either side of a bitter divide. The fault-line from the American epicentre simultaneously appeared in every conversation and province around the world, threatening to divide the communion as a whole. No ground was safe. Perhaps an embrace in the Southern African province would have brought a new perspective and the possibility of healing. Fresh thinking often comes after travel. Rowan Williams' attempts to calm hardened hearts covered the cracks but could not clear the rubble. He counselled against quick and irrevocable decisions as, on his watch, he was witnessing the Anglican Communion tearing itself apart, pulling left and right.

The then Archbishop of Nigeria opposed the conference as he was firmly on one side of the divide and saw that Ndungane had supported Gene Robinson and his consecration. The Nigerian Archbishop had called the consecration of Gene Robinson 'a Satanic attack'. Nigeria has a strong conservative Muslim population. Within his context the Nigerian Archbishop's response was in part to counter the claim that the Anglican church was liberal and western. He also stated that he would boycott a conference held in South Africa, and Desmond Tutu asked what all the fuss was about.[26]

Archbishop Rowan Williams was a man beleaguered. He felt he had little recourse but to host Lambeth, as always, in the UK. However, Williams attempted to bring a little of Africa to the conference by the use of South African discernment methodology, the system of indaba. This process was critiqued, and many of the bishops declined the invitation to come. The potential South African conference would have made a larger statement, which would have been to dislodge the shadow of a negative colonial past.

So what about Lambeth 2020 with Archbishop Welby? This time there was a huge push to include as many bishops as possible and their spouses. 'Get on board' was the overriding message coming from our smiling archbishop and wife on the Lambeth Conference website. There was one condition: not all spouses were welcome to attend. Bearing in mind that the ship of the Church of England is in such bad nick, is it any wonder that the biggest ship we have is also in poor repair? Perhaps the excluded spouses are better off not coming if the reception is going to be so cool. If you were a bishop in a same-sex relationship, your spouse was off the guest list. Blogger and priest New Yorker Winnie Varghese had a view on this and posted this response on her Facebook page, sharing a perspective from across the pond:

> I told an archbishop once that recent Lambeth conferences have done irreparable harm to the witness of The Episcopal Church to the most vulnerable in our society, poor, LGBTQI, POC, because if we show on the international stage that we won't love our own people and our own leaders and their families, how could we possibly love them/us. Here we go again. We should not do this anymore until we have leaders who have shaken off the colonial baggage of the false self-importance of Britishness and whiteness to save the rest of us from ourselves. If you can't invite everyone on equal terms, cancel. You're not ready. Delay, again … It appears that Lambeth itself might be the problem by creating the platform for schismatics to remain festering and divisive within the fold, visibly, at Lambeth. I will not say anything about the duplicitous cruelty of the C of E towards its own clergy because that is not my place, but we must not do the same to our people.[27]

So is it any wonder, if at the highest and widest level we are discriminating, that discrimination is found within the national church? Perhaps if we fix things at a global level, the national level will be adjusted. Perhaps. Are the Church of England's senior leaders and systems allowing the pain of discrimination to fester without ever truly dealing with it? If that is the case, brown and black people need each other more than ever.

Hinterland

1. The remote areas of a country away from the coast or the banks of major rivers.
2. The area around or beyond a major town or port.
3. An area lying beyond what is visible or known.[28]

Let's take another look at the early church community spoken of by Welby in his work, in this imagined episode based on the biblical narrative in the book of Acts.

After sunset, the young man entered the quiet home for his appointment. His night vision took in the shapes of sleeping children and the dimensions of the room, then a small figure detached itself from the darkness, appearing by his side. It was the children's mother; her thin fingers guided him to the ladder that led to the roof. They sat beside one another in silence for a moment under a canopy of stars, until her prolonged coughing interrupted the moment. He began his investigation: 'Are you okay?' The young man's gentle tone drew out the truth. The veiled woman shrank from his gaze. He patiently persisted: 'Please tell me what's wrong, maybe we can help.' She studied him, and trusted him. 'We are hungry, we haven't eaten in days. The little I can scavenge goes to my children.' Silence. He kept listening, until she began talking again, first in drips then in a torrent.

'I had thought the church would be a home for me and my children since my husband died in the emperor's war. I had thought this was a new society, where all were equal. Jesus is for everyone, but it seems he favours his own people, the Jews, more than us Gentiles. I had thought I would be included, like the others are.' The young man waited for what he knew was coming. 'The other women,' she whispered, 'the Jewish ones, every day they are served first. We are sent to the back of the queue, or told to return at a different time, but by the time we arrive there is nothing left. Nothing!' Her tears grew into sobs, and a child below also began to scream, snared in a nightmare. She slowed her breathing, the child below also settled. In the moonlight the man detected uncertainty in her eyes. 'Please don't say I told you. We have been told there are so many join-ing the community that they will ensure we are provided for. We just have to be patient they say. I don't want any trouble. I have lost my people through choosing Christ, this community is not perfect but it is all we have.' The man's cheeks were wet too. He spoke, 'Sister Zoe, our Lord said we should pray that we receive our daily bread. The Hebrew story of freedom and daily manna for the liberated slaves as they became a people not a possession, was the story Jesus was drawing on. We, you, are no one's but God's, and God sets you free, to give and receive. Trust me.' He was resolved, he had heard too many stories like this. The disciples were gathering, he had the evidence, he and his Greek companions would be challenging the disciples to expose this injustice and invite them to act to remedy this widespread problem.[29]

One ethnic group had power over another. One ethnic group was getting the lion's-share of the resources. With strength derived from ethnicity, the weak who were the 'them' were being left out. The established servers were part of the 'us' and leaving out the 'them'. There was not the infrastructure to accommodate all those joining. Some people were being left out. The Hebrew widows were getting preferential treatment, the Hellenist widows were starving. They were being neglected. The apostles were overwhelmed by this turn of events and had their focus fixed so much on the mission, this growing church, that they struggled to realise the vital maintenance work that needed to be done. The advocates for the widows were brilliantly brave.

Were the disciples a little too big for their boots? Was serving seen as beneath them, in that they would pray and preach but not apply plasters, or distribute rice? Or was something else going on? They said: 'Select from among yourselves.' This was like the vicar telling me to conduct a survey of the minority ethnic congregation. This could be the disciples recognising that there was an ongoing problem related to ethnicity, but with the humility to know that they could not solve it. The disciples go further, they gather the whole community and there is a clear transfer of power and positive affirmative action takes place. These new men are added to the group, they do not displace or replace the disciples.

If the Acts church is the model of community that society is to embrace, can we allow those of black and minority ethnic backgrounds to come together, to bring our pain, then receive the transfer of power to enact that change, and with this additional responsibility can we have additional resources? Can we come away by ourselves to be restored? This needs to be at all levels of the church and society. The black and brown clergy and laity have attempted to call for help. We have believed that the Church of England could be our hinterland. The Committee for Minority Ethnic Concerns, perceiving the difference in treatment black and brown clergy and laity received in comparison with their elite white English counterparts, like sister Zoe in the narrative claimed their right to equal treatment. This was packaged in a 2015 report called *I too am C of E*. It was an attempt to establish the connection with all God's children. There was hope that people of colour would be seen as valid, vital and valued members of the church they loved. But for black and brown members of the clergy and laity the Church of England in its current form cannot be our hinterland. The debate was painful. Even those senior leaders who are on the way can still get tongue-tied. General Synod was in session and the Bishop of Chelmsford, now Archbishop of York, had been part of the Committee for Minority Ethnic Concerns, he had been exposed to the impact of structural bias on black and brown people. He said in response to the report:

The leadership and ministry of the C of E no longer looks like or adequately reflects the diversity or creativity of the community it serves ... It directly affects our credibility as a national church and our mission.

This is well known, and well said to his peers. Later in his speech he said that the church

may not be guilty of racism. But it is time to be clear and honest with ourselves, there is still racism in our Church. It is high time we woke up out of our sleep and realise we are guilty of complacency and neglect.

He commented that the situation had got worse over the past 30 years, which again points back to that moment in time when the *Faith in the City* report was published. 'The statistics tell us we are going backwards,' he said, 'not because we are racists, but because we have just not faced up and taken affirmative action.'[30]

It makes me wonder how the church 'may not be guilty of racism', and yet 'there is racism in our church'. Racism is helpfully dissociated from the senior white leadership, relocated to some back office with large filing cabinets bulging with all the other reports the committee has produced. But can there be affirmative action without affirmative contrition? Can there be sorrow, and an all-out attack on the (Club) – a deliberate weakening of unjust power?

The former Archbishop of York, Dr Sentamu, said he was 'too long in the tooth' on this issue. 'I don't have the passion of the Bishop of Chelmsford, but I am glad that we were separated at birth. I used to speak on this issue with the same passion.' Indeed, in November 2019, after announcing his retirement and ahead of an Advent resource being launched, he found that passion. He roared again about racism in the church but unsurprisingly his powerful words went largely unheard. When black and brown clergy cry institutional racism they are seen as weak and ungrateful, even if they have been at the receiving end. When white clergy call it out they are seen as strong and generous even if they have been part of the problem.

Back to the debate in 2015.

As the discussion developed, Dr Elizabeth Henry, the black academic and national advisor directing CMEAC, picked up the conversation and spelt out the point in no uncertain terms:

Where racism exists in our church, whether institutional or personal, and/or where unconscious bias occurs, we should be challenging it and should be calling it. Do we have the nerve and the strength to challenge it wherever we see it?[31]

Well, now a senior white leader has said that racism does exist – so it does.

But as the Bishop of Chelmsford demonstrates, it can be an uncomfortable topic. What became of the Bishop of Chelmsford?

Two years later, in 2017, we find him in the hallowed halls of the House of Lords responding to a government audit on racial disparity: 'My Lords, although, let me be clear, the Church of England has nothing to teach anyone else on this subject – our record is not a good one.'

I think he could have ended his speech there. But he went on.

In the diocese of Chelmsford, where I serve, which includes the east London boroughs, which have some of the most diverse communities in Europe, we have found that of course there is racism and xenophobia but there is also what has been explained to me as unconscious bias.

He continued:

It [unconscious bias] is not quite the same as racism; it is those things which prevent us from seeing each other as clearly as we need to. Both in the Church of England generally and in the diocese where I serve, we have done a lot of training over the past couple of years to help people to see their own unconscious bias towards people ... I wondered whether the Government had looked at that both for us and in wider society to try to move the debate on beyond the binary thing of: 'Somebody is a racist or they are not'.[32]

In the book *White Fragility* the white thinker and diversity coach Robin DeAngelo suggests that white people only see racism as the extremely ugly stuff: obvious name calling, racial slurs, and lynchings and beatings. Bald-headed, goose-stepping, angry white men. With that as the benchmark, it is indeed a 'binary thing'. How many of my readers would identify with that description? Yet in *White Fragility* DeAngelo gives another definition that includes when one has the power over another to impact their lives and chances, when one maintains a status quo to the exclusion of others and at the expense of them flourishing.[33] Others delineate racism as a type of pollution which affects us all. Unconscious bias training in and of itself is a form of unconscious bias.

The question is, now that we all know that institutional racism exists, how can the Church of England be the hinterland for black and brown clergy? I have already mentioned the AMEN network of Anglican clergy; I am excited about this. It is a positive example of the advocates in Acts coming together and finding a hinterland.

In the Hebrew Scriptures there is a story of a prophet called Elijah; he is isolated and exhausted from seeking to overturn the system of oppression caused by the king, Ahab, and his wife Jezebel, who has a team of prophets who worship gods of death. The syncretism between Ahab and Jezebel has polluted the ethics and the values of God's people.

Elijah declares a climate emergency and there are three years of drought. This disturbs the populace and unsettles the powers that be. Eventually all the institutions marshalled by Jezebel come out against him for a showdown. The public are watching, the earth is parched, but before the rain must come the fire. Fire from heaven that consumes and incinerates the sacrifice, destroys the edifice, scorching the earth, clearing the way for the new. This leads to a mass repentance and then to the extermination of the systems of oppression. Then comes the rain. However, Elijah is not part of a society of activists. He's a lone ranger, and with the heavy clouds descends a heavy mood and he runs for his life.

Medusa's snakes have been decapitated but Medusa's

head remains in place. From bloody stumps the serpents will re-emerge and seek their vengeance. Jezebel is angry and seeks Elijah out; she cannot find him, but the silent assassin of depression does the pursuing and overtakes him. Elijah feels lost, alone and afraid. He has challenged the powers, he has won this battle, but the war is ongoing and the hissing of the snakes torments his waking dreams. A number of global majority clergy feel like this.

The colleges, the communities, congregations and cathedrals, and the Cross and the Crown (Club), are all at best only responsive if people of colour call for help, and at worst are complicit in the suffering of people of colour. There is nowhere to go and no one to listen who is able to hear and understand our plight, and aid us in our fight. It is exhausting justifying, describing, explaining, and complaining about one's sense of oppression. We need to hear the similarities of our journeys to give a sense of solidarity. We need that. Elijah eventually ends up in a cave and hears the 'still small voice of God' telling him he is not alone. Sometimes it is not about Turning Up the Volume, but about turning down the background noise. Elijah empowers others to cut out the rot at the root and replace the current kingdom; it's bloody and messy, but to be a new beginning, one needs an effective and decisive ending. This time it is Medusa's head that is removed from her person. Her snakes gasp for a source of oxygen which is no more. After this Elijah gets a partner who has a whole school of prophets speaking truth to power and a movement is underway. One of my hopes about this book is that it will spark a sense of solidarity across global majority Anglicans. But we cannot wait for the system to dismantle itself. We have to do it ourselves. We need a hinterland.

What an exodus and early church community inspired by Elijah might look like

What follows is a small way in which a few of us took a small step forward. Myself and other clergy of colour attended the priesting of a couple of friends in another diocese. There were three people priested that day; two were clergy of colour, one was white. We came away delighted for our friends but frustrated with the service. We decided to address our concerns to the bishop, here is the correspondence, with names changed.

Dear +Archibald,

We are a collection of black clergy from the diocese of xxxx. Below are the concerns to raise with you. Each of the points we make has been carefully considered and it is important they are taken seriously. This is an opportunity to review policies and procedures and make amendments that will not just mitigate the hurt experienced when minorities are excluded, but enrich these celebrations for everyone.

When two thirds of the candidates are from the very demographic that our Archbishops and senior leadership purport to want above all, the service spoke an opposite message. There was a white man also and the service felt as if it were designed only with him in mind.

The Cross and Candles:
A white male carried the cross with two young black women carrying the candles. One of the black candle bearers could have carried the cross to demonstrate that, as two-thirds of the candidates were of BAME stock, this was noticed, and celebrated. Again we stress the importance of visual messages. This ceremony appeared as if it was designed around the white male.

The Losses:
When we arrived it was wonderful to see so many BAME clergy, congregation, and such a lot of young people, as well

as children. The opportunity for a recruitment drive was a clear and present reality. Unfortunately the messages many of our black communities already hold about the church were upheld: The church is not designed with us in mind, it is not designed with us in its heart, that position is reserved for the white male.

Did the curates and their training incumbents have the opportunity to shape the service design? Did they feel represented and heard? Or was this a tried-and-tested template designed for white men, and then applied to everyone as the normal standard?

Did anyone investigate that the worship acknowledged the depth and breadth of the heritage and music tradition that affirmed all the candidates fullest and highest sense of identity?

Sermon:
During the sermon, the preacher, your Archdeacon, could have given up their right to speak and offered the sermon to a black clergy person. That would have been significant.

As for the white male candidate, celebrating his peers' fullest sense of self would not have diminished his own experience. Rather it would have enriched it and shown him the type of diocese and church he is joining.

Speaking parts:
We counted at least ten black clergy, competent and capable of speaking up and out. We invite you to consider how it might feel to be in our place. We are distressed that, yet again, the black members were the silent members. The trope of the quiet person in the 'black'ground runs deep through our recent colonial and slave histories. That the service could be designed without one black person uttering words of prayer, or bringing a reading, is insensitive and offensive.

Now the readers of scripture were all white, but the candidates were two-thirds black. Whatever the reasons for white readers, and however it is usually done, this of all occasions was a great opportunity to take another look and actually see who was there, and what they represented, and who should be called on to represent them. We understand there can be an argument of setting a precedent. (name of Diocese) is a place we thought was keen to do just that.

What is the response? Will this contribute to a rethink, and possible reworking of the services?

Regards
xxxxx secretary of xxxxx and other members who preferred to remain anonymous

...

Dear Revd X, and through you the other contributors, named and anonymous

I am now able to say thank you for bringing this up with me. We do not know each other personally, and I don't know what your experience has been of previous interactions with senior clergy. Speaking personally, the encouragement of an open and inclusive church for all who have been marginalised is at the heart of my personal faith and has been central to my ministry. Your email was therefore difficult reading. It took me some time to disentangle the important points you wanted to raise from the rather combative tone in which they were expressed, and the emotional response that it created.

Before replying, I shared your message with both Tony and Stephanie [the black ordinands], and have met with them this morning, and discussed the service, and how I might respond. To be clear, this is my response in the light of that conversation. Firstly, I must acknowledge that there is something for me to learn from your critique. As Tony said in our meeting this morning, when nothing else is explicitly celebrated, the majority identity is. I should have given thought to that fact, rather than assuming that the format and structure of the service as it has normally been conducted at the (name of place) was sufficient.

Secondly, I was delighted and relieved that neither Tony

nor Stephanie felt excluded during the service. The contrast with your experience maybe illustrates the difference that personal relationships make to the experience. We all have work to do to enable the Church of England to reflect its diversity, and to celebrate it. Please pray for me as I seek to do so.

Best wishes

+Archibald

Here was our thought. We were from another diocese travelling to see our friends in their Dire-Seas. We were outside their system and felt we could share what we felt and saw. Being part of a different diocesan structure enabled and emboldened us to speak on Tony and Stephanie's behalf, though we could not speak to our own bishops in that way. But being from a different diocese and working as a collective offered some protection. I signed the first letter along with a few other signatories and had the line 'anonymous others', as some preferred to keep their identities private. When the response was penned, another member of the group drafted it and signed off as secretary to lessen the risk for me, and demonstrate a collective unit.

Unanticipated problems and opportunities arising from this ...

There is always the tension between integration and separation. People crudely describe MLK as wanting to integrate with the system and Malcolm X as wanting to separate from the system and people of colour wanting to develop their own power base and resources. There was a split in the thinking of the group from which our group arose. Were we a campaigning group, or any kind of group? Should we send such a potentially inflammatory letter, or should we rather seek a meeting and try and reason? Others of us thought we ought to lob a grenade in, from the safety of another place and as part of a crowd, and let the people in the place build things up the right way. In fact, when Tony heard about the letter, he contacted me saying 'You lot are like Malcolm (X) highlighting the issue, and now me and Stephanie have to be Martin, and involved in resolving the issues.'

With the story of Elijah the drought proved that the leadership was powerless to help. Even if you are in the minority, you first confront with the fire, then dismantle the system, then the rain of reconciliation can come.

The action was inspired by the Association of Black Clergy (ABC) – a powerful expression of unity across the various denominations of the church. As the prophets prove, you cannot do this by yourselves, you need a team. It was more than a get-together, it had clarity and purpose. Wilfred Wood was chair of the ABC close to its origin. And among the many achievements, they would meet and both travel to ordinations and installations en masse, and advocate for other suffering clergy by sending letters or putting together a little delegation who would meet the senior leader to show support for their wounded colleagues.

Notes

1 Selby, P. (1991), *Belonging: Challenge to a Tribal Church*, London: SPCK.

2 Ibid., p. 13.

3 Ibid.

4 www.independent.co.uk/news/uk/home-news/justin-welby-church-of-england-windrush-racism-christianity-a9330606.html.

5 Welby, J. (2018), *Reimagining Britain*, London: Bloomsbury. Preface.

6 Ibid., p. 32.

7 Ibid.

8 Italics mine.

9 Welby, *Reimagining Britain*, p. 33.

10 Ibid.

11 Beckford, R. (2000), 'Doing Black Theology in the UKKK', *Black Theology: An International Journal* 4: 38–60, p. 53.

12 Ibid.

13 http://archive.southwark.anglican.org/thebridge/0002/page14. htm.

14 Beckford, 'Doing', p. 53.

15 Isiorho, D. (2002), 'Black Theology in Urban Shadow: Combating Racism in the Church of England', *Black Theology: An International Journal*, Vol. 1, No. 1: 29–48, p. 47.

16 Welby, *Reimagining Britain*, p. 33.

17 Ibid., p. 11.

18 Ibid., p. 33.

19 Ibid., p. 34.

20 Ibid., p. 96.

21 Ibid.

22 Ibid.

23 Lewis, Harold T. (2007), *A Church for the Future, South Africa as the Crucible for Anglicanism in the New Century*, New York: Church Publishing, p. 5.

24 Ibid.

25 Ibid.

26 Ibid., p. 6.

27 Winnie Varghese, Saturday 16 February 2019.

28 *Oxford English Dictionary*.

29 A retelling of Acts 6.1–8.

30 *Church Times* (2020), 'Statistics on BAME priests in senior posts are shocking'. Available online at: www.churchtimes.co.uk/articles/2015/17-july/news/uk/statistics-on-bame-priests-in-senior-posts-are-shocking.

31 Ibid.

32 The Church of England in Parliament (2020), *Bishop of Chelmsford responds to Government statement on race disparity audit*. Available online at: https://churchinparliament.org/2017/10/10/bishop-of-chelmsford-responds-to-government-statement-on-race-disparity-audit/.

33 DeAngelo, R. (2019), *White Fragility*, London: Allen Lane.

7

You Cannot Judge a Book
by its Cover

Throughout this book we have been exploring concepts of being black and what whiteness might mean. We have spent much of our time looking backwards. In this next section I introduce you to two friends who complicate the categories. First we meet David, and then second we will meet Hannah.

Some people are proudly English in heart and soul. The following conversation I had with an old friend spelt out how even the most English of us, in ideals and identity, can struggle to integrate into the Church of England system of discernment, let alone go through to ordination. The vessels cannot even accommodate my friend David.

London's government City Hall was the grand backdrop of my interview with a high-ranking politician within his party. He met me, this man mountain, with a broad smile, salt-and-pepper beard and a twinkle in his eyes. He greeted me with a warm handshake and then showed me around the stunning feat of architecture that is City Hall. Our tour of City Hall was repeatedly interrupted by other politicians wanting to button-hole him, getting his reaction to an emerging issue; and in our numerous lift journeys someone would strike up a conversation with him. It was clear to me he was comfortable with those we encountered. He took time to talk with and listen to staff as well as peers. He and I were old friends, together for a season back in the early 2000s in a trendy church. As well as a common church background, he, like me, has a West Indian heritage, though his white English mother raised him, as black Jamaican dad was not around. He identifies with his white heritage.

I asked David if he was born and raised in the UK.

I was born in West Sussex. My mum's English, my dad was Jamaican, I grew up with my mum and grandparents, I never met my dad as he left before I was born. To all intents and purposes, culturally I'm English, I'm British.

I asked if he had had any connection with Jamaica and he described a couple of visits he had made. His first trip was a fact-finding trip. He made some enquiries about his father's family. The search proved fruitless but he had a surprise he wasn't expecting: 'It was a shock, I knew I was half-Jamaican. I thought I was going to fit in, but the people of the Island saw me as a foreigner – you know: someone different. I didn't fit in as a native which I thought I would.' I shared a similar experience of a trip to Nevis, where I felt like an outsider. Now as I write, I reflect on when I was 15 years old and had spent time with my father. It was he who offered me access to the Island by explaining who was who, and how I fitted into the larger picture of relations. My father had provided introductions that helped foster that aspect of my identity. David had no such familial catalyst to help him feel at home. I asked David on a scale of one to ten how conscious he was of his black heritage:

It's not something I think about much at all, I am who I am. I suppose I think about it sometimes, on that scale, I'd say three or four perhaps. These days people are talking so much about identity politics. Years ago I wouldn't notice skin colours, I would interact, just person to person ... These days people like to think of themselves belonging to a group and not as an individual. Personally I liked it when I was a student 20 years ago and everyone was just a person.

This statement connects with the discussion on colour blindness. David then shared something of which I took particular note. He said: 'It's interesting, I've just done one of these gene tests you can have done, and it came out 60 per cent European and 40 per cent West African, that's going back 500 years when Jamaicans were in Africa.'

Knowing something of David's convictions on his formation and foundation being English, I asked him if that knowledge had changed the way he saw himself. 'It does a bit, I'm actually very happy with that because it means I am more European than I am Jamaican African, which fits in with my upbringing. Somewhere in my father's line is German. My last name is German. I understand I have more European heritage in my genes, which is what I feel like as a person.'

Harold Lewis, the black Episcopalian priest, charts the emergence of Caribbean ministry in America in the late nineteenth century. His delineation of their arrival, it could be suggested, has parallels with David's preferring his white side over the dark side. Lewis speaks of superiority and a confidence in these West Indian ministers when he states:

> They believed that their superiority stemmed from their Englishness, having been immersed in an educational system predicated on the concept of the British imperium, which stressed the inherent superiority of the English over the rest of the world.

David's blackness has lost out in favour of his white English identity. Nevertheless, two trips to Jamaica and a recent gene test show a search for a deeper understanding. Like the Caribbean ministers discussed by Lewis, David, without ready access to his Caribbean heritage, has still adopted and internalised an English preference within his own person as his Caribbean forebears had done. David and I then moved to the nub of the conversation. I was curious as to how an emerging desire and willingness to explore ordained ministry was snuffed out:

> I attended one of the church courses. Some people said 'Would you like to run this course next time?' I didn't see myself as someone who would get actively involved in any sort of Christian ministry. But I thought, 'Okay, I've been asked, and people had confidence in me,' so I did and got very good feedback regarding my leadership in that small area. Then people encouraged me, they suggested: 'Why don't you train

to be in the ministry, to become a vicar?' I thought about it, I wasn't sure but decided to approach the vicar and see what he would say. He dissuaded me from doing it actually.

Before David moved on, I asked 'On what grounds were you dissuaded?' He continued:

The vicar had a specific idea. He said: 'There are three types of people: some are Adventurers, some are Carers, and some are Teachers. Which two would you describe yourself most as?' I said, 'Probably a Carer first and then a Teacher.' He said, 'Thanks for being honest, but we need people who are Adventurers. We need people who are project managers who can do stuff. The church is full of Carers and Teachers, so I would advise you not to do it because you'd be very nice, but you're not the sort of person the church needs.' That was his perspective.

I asked David how that left him feeling:

I was disappointed at the time because I thought vicars were supposed to be pastoral, and caring and pass on knowledge and teach in order to develop people. He had his view, but that was how it was at the time. I am actually very glad now, sitting here 15 years later.

I was saddened that after several stages of encouragement David's flame of interest was extinguished by one strong voice, and one opinion. A reductionist homemade personality matrix was applied, and David was discounted. I also sat in front of the same vicar and had the same speech before I began working with him on his staff team for a spell. I fortunately had said 'Adventurer' in my list. I had no idea it was a 'sorting hat'. The vicar claimed divine guidance, yet his crude methodology was arbitrarily designed to replicate himself within his team. A few years later, when I desired opportunities to serve in the church and test whether I should consider it as a vocation, I had this speech from the vicar, which at the time I did not read as a snub:

I have a number of people wanting to be ordained so can't rota you into services, but if you can find another church that will give you the opportunities to preach, teach and lead, I'll support that.

He held such a place in my estimation that I followed orders. I deferred to his assumed greater wisdom. So I left the church and my job, took my wife and found a church in another area, and I am grateful that the white vicar there went out of his way to accommodate us. He managed to create a role, source funding and if it were not for him, I too might have been dissuaded. What I had thought in the former church was a beginning – I imagined serving alongside the vicar I respected – turned out to be an ending.

This is a huge problem. All clergy are actively encouraged, press-ganged even, into fanning the flame of even the slightest spark from possible black and minority ethnic candidates. I have sat in rooms consulting with Ministry Division (the department within the church which manages and monitors the recruitment process to ordained ministry from vocations days, to theological college, to the point of ordination and beyond). In these conversations, there is concern that although there are recruitment drives at diocese level, the vicars are the gatekeepers. They control the flow of information. But maybe David had a lucky escape. At the time of writing David is a politician with UKIP. How could UKIP have seen potential in a way the Church of England as represented by one of its priests was blind to? How could they have offered quicker opportunities and a warmer welcome? Then again when I tell many people my role and vocation they seem as surprised that I am a vicar as I was when I learned that David was in UKIP. So perhaps David and I are on equally precarious ships?

When I began my ministry in the Church of England I had some vibrant colleagues to work and train with, and one of these was a young white English woman called Hannah Johnston.

Me   What are some of your early memories and encounters in thinking about ethnicity and race. That of your own and others?

Hannah   The town that I grew up in, in the 1980s was probably about 99.9 per cent white at the time, so in terms of personal encounters I don't remember many from my childhood. My first memory of race and ethnicity was wanting to have a bright green Granny Smith's apple from the greengrocers when I was probably six or seven. My mum said no because they were from South Africa and my parents were boycotting South African goods, because of apartheid, and she explained what that meant.

Me   I'm going to skip ahead. When you were training for ordination what in your theological education addressed race and ethnicity, in the culture of the college or in the taught curriculum?

Hannah   So I'm struggling to think of anything that addressed it directly. My college was overwhelmingly white. After I moved to New York in the third year, they did have one session about race and ethnicity that I wasn't present for [Hannah left England mid-course and completed her third year as a distance learner.] We touched on liberation theology briefly in one lecture, but in terms of other theologies, I don't think we ever talked about black liberation theology. Certainly I never heard about womanist theology until I moved to the US.

Me   And what was it like working with a black person – me? Were there any reservations or hesitations either in yourself or in those around you when they heard who you were with?

Hannah   I didn't really think about the fact that I had not worked with many black people before, as I had lived in white places almost my whole life before going to live in London. Working with you was key in being able to start to picture myself being in church leadership. Both you, and Emily, who I then worked for in New York, were the first church leaders that I knew who weren't middle-aged white men, and who didn't lead in a top-down pyramid model, 'alpha male' way. You were the first person that I came across that had ideas about collaborative leadership. And I think at first I struggled with that idea, because it was so foreign to what I had been told was the only way to do things. But it made me realise that that was one of the things that was holding me back from being able to picture myself being a leader. I thought I would have to become a different person – some kind of scheduled and organised white alpha-male person.

I particularly liked the church notice-board we had. I always come back to your design of that notice-board every time I go to churches and I see their very neat little structures with their pastor at the top, and their elders below them, and the deacons below them. Those churches show the hierarchy. I remember the notice-board at our church said 'We are all ministers'. I loved that the board was filled with little pictures of all of us in the congregation displayed in no particular order. That layout had a real impact on me. And then when I worked with Emily at St Lydia's in New York, she is a white woman and led differently from men. I think the combination of both working for you and then working for her were really formative for me.

Me   So can you tell me what it was about moving to New York which introduced or developed your thinking about race and ethnicity, your own and that of others?

Hannah   My introduction to race and racism as a theory and a system has come mostly from the US, a little bit from the South African context through reading as a teenager and through watching movies. I always had this picture in my mind that America was more racist than the UK, which I think a lot of UK people have, and I think the biggest learning for me was that I don't think that is true, I just think it manifests differently.

When I was first in New York, I very much thought, 'Oh yes, this is so much worse, because everything is more extreme and more in-your-face,' and I moved there the month that Eric Garner was killed in New York. Emily started preaching a lot about race and racism and about the Black Lives Matter movement.

So I think over that season between moving to New York and getting really involved and working with Emily at St Lydia's, the congregation had been on a number of Black Lives Matter marches. I also got involved with Faith in New York, an inter-faith community-organising network. It was hosted by large primarily black congregations around New York who have big beautiful buildings and a long history of community-organising work. I started to see that history a lot more. It was also interesting how much more segregated everything in the US seemed to be, particularly places of worship. If people of colour were excluded from white denominations then they had no other choice but to develop their own denominations. Those churches have grown into amazing, safe, supportive, deeply theological, transformative communities.

Me   You mentioned with the community-organising, that there was an expectation that the white organisers would have their own group to consider the ideology of whiteness. I'm curious about how that was presented to you and how you came to understand it?

Hannah   One of the Faith in New York staff invited me to join a 'white affinity group' he was starting. He explained that when the wider staff had been on a retreat together, one afternoon there was an opportunity for people of colour to gather in affinity groups to support one another. The white people didn't know what to do with themselves during that time slot, and sort of wandered aimlessly on the beach. The Executive Director of Faith in New York at the time (an African American woman) challenged him to get the white people together in their own group and talk about whiteness and interrogate that. He invited Emily and I and some other white faith leaders to be a part of this group. We always struggled to find a name for it so we informally called it the 'Awkward White People' group! But what was really interesting was thinking about whiteness, asking each other questions like the sort of questions you asked me, like 'What were your first encounters with your own race or other people's race?' And just being really honest with each other about ways that we've messed up in the past, ideals that we had, for example 'Oh I will be that white person that stands up against the racists' and then when the moment comes you don't. I think most of us were probably already involved in inter-racial, inter-faith work in some way. I did wonder at the time if I could do something like this in the UK. Who would I invite? Who do I think is thinking in these ways? And I did feel that there would be a lot more pushback, that people wouldn't necessarily acknowledge that there was a problem in the UK. That is one of the things that I've noticed when I've tried to talk to people back in the UK about the type of work I've done in the US. There is this assumption: 'Oh yes the US is super racist but we're not like that in the UK.'

When I did the Community Organiser training, the national training with Faith in New York's national organisation (The PICO Network), I began thinking about racism as a structure for the first time, rather than just personal prejudice, and the conclusion that I came to is that racism exists just as much in the UK but that it is more hidden. I guess everything in the US is more extreme anyway, the country is bigger, the weather is more extreme, the extremes of poverty and wealth is more extreme, the food portions are more extreme; everything there is more extreme. There is more violence because their gun laws are different and police carry guns, and racial difference in poverty and poor health are more extreme because of a less comprehensive welfare state and lack of public healthcare, and maybe explicit racism is more extreme – particularly historically and in the south. But there is also more representation and opportunity for people of colour. For example, black British actors move to Hollywood because they can get parts there that they can't get in the UK. And it is easy to find children's books and greetings cards that feature people of colour in a way that you can't in the UK. The conclusion that I came to is that in the UK racism is masked by a lot of things, including British reserve and a veneer of 'politeness', and the same racist attitudes exist, they are just a lot more hidden.

Me   Thank you. I imagine going to New York you were able to begin to supplement your English theological education with black and liberative theologies. How did that help you to begin to engage with the topics in a new way?

Hannah   What has been transformative is the double lens of queer theology and womanist theology. I came across them partly through St Lydia's church in New York, and partly through a training course which had an intersectional approach to justice work. Anti-racism work was inherently connected to undoing homophobia and through understanding Bible texts in alternative ways. I was exposed to a lot of writing around racial justice and my cohort was a hugely diverse bunch of people.

Probably the most key person to me was Dr

Cheryl Anderson, an African American woman who is Professor of Old Testament at Garrett-Evangelical Theological Seminary. She introduced me to a different way of doing biblical interpretation. She spoke about the distinction between exegesis and eisegesis. She argues that people are often taught at seminary that exegesis is interpreting scripture correctly and drawing out what God has to say, and eisegesis is that the interpreter makes the text say what they want it to say. The assumption being the first one is good and is objective and the second one is subjective and it is inadequate. Her thesis is that this distinction is a false one. That there is no such thing as a neutral or unbiased interpretation of scripture. What we have been taught for hundreds of years as the 'correct' interpretations of scripture are based around the needs and worldviews of powerful white, heterosexual, western men.

And that the impact of this perspective is terrible for women, for people of colour, for queer people, for poor people and non-western people, and anyone that doesn't fit into this kind of 'mythical norm'. She argues for interpreting scripture from the viewpoint of the marginalised, to develop an alternative exegesis. She was probably the first womanist scholar that I encountered in person.

Me   So I am curious to know, what has it been about queer theology that has shone a light on racial justice?

Hannah   It has really been in coming to understand the concept of 'intersectionality', a term that was coined by Kimberlé Crenshaw. The idea that when people carry multiple oppressions they are more marginalised, which makes perfect sense to me. I also started to notice how much the LGBTQ+ community and agenda is dominated by white cis gay men. I went to a conference which was for LGBTQ+ Christians, but looking at the line-up on stage it was as if they had taken the straight white men you 'normally' see on stage at a Christian event and just replaced them with gay white men!

Being part of St Lydia's was not only the first fully affirming LGBTQ church that I was a part of, but it also had 'We are Queer' as one of the foundational identities of the church. So it was: We are Christian, We are Lutheran, We are Dinner Church, We are Queer, We seek Justice and We are Neighbours.

So 'We are Queer' didn't mean that every member of our church identified as LGBTQ+ but it meant that we were committed to challenging false binaries, like female and male, insider or outsider, believer or non-believer, things like that, but also we were constantly looking to the margins and seeing what the Holy Spirit was doing on the margins. And ensuring that a diversity of voices were being heard from the pulpit so that it wasn't just the white lady pastor that was preaching every week. That queer people were being listened to, that black people were being listened to, even in what was an overwhelmingly white congregation, making an effort always to be turning outwards, not turning in on ourselves and becoming insular. To be gearing everything that we did to the newcomer and trying not to use insider language. This made me think about a lot of things differently.

Me   I'm wondering, so you grew up in an area that was 99 point-something white and often the argument is – well this is an interesting conversation if you live in London or Birmingham or Manchester but for the Church of England for most of England it's just not a relevant conversation. Why should white people care in rural areas and areas where it's more ethnically monochrome?

Hannah   In the light of Brexit we can't pretend any more that the UK isn't racist. In the light of everything that has happened with Meghan and Harry and all that has come out about the racism she's experienced constantly since moving to the UK, we cannot pretend any more that this is not an issue. And every church should be responding to that. I definitely think there is a place for mostly white communities examining themselves. I also think however white and rural a community is, there will be isolated people of colour living within them. I read an article the other day from a black woman living in an overwhelmingly white area and she said, 'I am drowning in whiteness.' She was talking about all the micro-aggressions she has to experience on a daily basis like people touching her hair or asking 'Where are you really from?' or telling her 'You're very articulate. You don't sound black.' Everyone has a responsibility, particularly Christians, to examine their church spaces and their community spaces and ask the questions: If a person of colour walks in here how would they experience us? Would the church be somewhere they could feel safe, for example show up with natural hair and not have everyone come over and start touching it? Or would they try our church for a few weeks and just get exhausted by having to interact with us and not come back?

Hannah's comment reminded me of when I attended the consecration of Rose Hudson-Wilkin as Bishop of Dover. At the close of the service I was walking alongside New Yorker Indian priest Winnie Varghese. A white male priest friend, who is usually pretty awake to matters of race, in fact he played a role in helping me navigate ordination, came up to me and began rubbing my head and hair saying: 'Oh I like your hair!' I was so surprised I was dumbfounded. I might have attempted to return the favour but, alas, he was follicly challenged. I took note that he did not attempt the same move on Winnie.

Me One of my white female friends said to me, 'How can I be an ally?' And the question that came into my mind was, 'Can she be an ally?'

Hannah I have thought about this from at least three different perspectives. First: being an ally to the LGBTQ+ community, which I have tried to be for the last 20 years. This would mean speaking out when people use 'gay' as an insult, for instance, in the more conservative spaces that I used to move in, and gently pushing back against people expressing homophobic views.

Then, second, over the last few years I've been thinking about how to be an ally to people of colour. It's hard. I've heard people say 'You are only as much of an ally as your last action. You have to recommit to it every day.' I'm also a big fan of the idea that everyone is going to make mistakes doing this kind of work, and that you just have to get used to messing up and apologising and moving on, and trying to do better.

And third, I have also thought about it as a woman. I think, 'How would I like a straight white man to speak up in defence of women, if misogynistic and sexist behaviour is taking place?' Then I try to enact that behaviour myself on behalf of other people. When men are saying misogynistic things it is so exhausting having to constantly have those arguments with those men, and it takes so much emotion out of you, I find it so helpful when guys will jump in and lend their support.

I'm trying to be that ally for the groups I have mentioned. I have tried to be the person that jumps in so that the people of colour, and queer people don't have to do that emotional labour all the time. I also think that, as a white person I am going to be in the room when other white people are saying something racist and there are no people of colour around. I am always asking myself, am I willing to speak up in those spaces and say 'That's not okay' and push back against it.

I think one of the other things about allyship is making an effort to educate yourself and not constantly asking people of colour to do the work for you. Or if one person of colour says something that challenges you or makes you feel uncomfortable or guilty, not running to your other friends of colour saying, 'Oh this person said this to me. It's not true is it?' – so much of that is white fragility. When things are said that make you feel angry, upset or guilty the thing to do is to take a step back and process that without spewing it all back to the person of colour.

Me   Hannah, thank you so much for this conversation.

The Church of England is not feeling 'safe', or 'easy', and a number of people of colour do not feel 'respect'. Yet we volunteer and are invited to join in. There are some settings that feel like compelling Golden Ticket churches, but in a factory there are only bosses and workers. In a factory church white leaders exploit black labour.

8

Buried Alive

Headway

I used to wear dreadlocks,
to unlock the historical blocks
of ancestral memory,
to show I was free,
like Marley, emancipated
from mental slavery,
Male slaves, heads shaved,
long haired Samson was weakened by the
barber's knife, hair left to grow
signalled powers reprise,
Samson got his hair back
but sacrificed his eyes,
although blind
he could see through the lies,
as the Philistines temple
came crashing down about his head,
his people were liberated,
their hero was dead.

BraveSlave[1]

Samson the rebel leader

In the introductory poem there is reference to the character Samson. An analysis of his story is a helpful lens through which to view the effect of someone subjugated to a dominant aggressor. This is not the book to interrogate the historicity or otherwise of this ancient strong man, and warrior chief of the Hebrew Scriptures. My task here is to revisit his story and identify themes to shed light on my experience and the experience of others. I am reading back as if Samson were a rebellious black slave who was strangely compelled by the power of the oppressor. In this retelling, the Philistines are the slaver class.

The Philistine god was called Dagon, worshipped in several temples, the temples representing the heart of their enterprise and source of their worldview of supremacy over the surrounding nations. Samson was not a passive participant in their system of oppression. He challenged their established order and his victories threw Dagon's power into question, and therefore the whole worldview into question. Samson destabilised the Philistines' ability to fully dominate their subject people. The Philistines could punish the bodies of the Israelites, but their minds could not be as easily broken. Samson and his legend infused his people's imagination with hope.

In the annals of the transatlantic slave trade, there are a number of stories of resistance which were met with overwhelming counter-force, but the bubbling rebellion and desire for liberation was always resurgent. Samson represents the indomitable spirit of the guerrilla fighter who has mastered their fear and is ready to do battle. The Philistines were unable to break his body in open combat so they changed tactic. They exploited his passion and his curiosity about their ways, and their women. A weakness of Samson, it seems, was a desire for power and validation. His heart was not set on 'a nice girl from his own people' as his mother wanted, but on one of the Philistine girls and the associated power and presumed access.

Samson's land is littered with the oppressors and Samson believes he deserves to marry one of them. He is aware of his personal power but seemingly unaware of his social standing. We all know this will not go well. His people are hated by the Philistines, yet the passage seems to indicate that God is implicated in Samson's attempt to integrate into the power base. A methodology to break slaves was to demolish family units. Samson tears, is torn away, from his community while believing in his sense of agency and free choice. He has a failed marriage attempt which leads to problems before he encounters Delilah who is a pawn of masters behind the scenes.

The exposure of the black clergy

Clergy of colour from impoverished blackgrounds can be drawn to white spaces to minister, feeling a sense of destiny, agency and compulsion. The leading of God is at play. There can be a desire to break out of the confinement of the situations they have come from. In my story, my mother was encouraging me to break free of my roots and penetrate the world around me. What is lost, however, is vital connection to the old story, which is necessary to sustain you. My mother equated Christianity with the English culture she encountered. She was surrounded by well-meaning white Christians who reinforced their unassessed cultural norms, creating a thick relational and cultural insulation around her. This in turn unwittingly severed some of her connection with her heritage. I too sought to find myself in an English Christian story but lost myself instead. When you are uprooted you begin to wilt.

The Philistines obtained Samson's acquiescence by using the weapon of distraction packaged in the form of the delightful Delilah. Delilah is responding to the offer of silver. A woman in those times had few options for earning a living. Delilah acts as a high-class escort with whom Samson is infatuated. We will return to Delilah.

In Samson's earlier attempt at marrying into the power base, the woman's father surrounds Samson with 30 Philistines 'companions'. All is going well, he has his 'companions', they are all in high spirits, Samson thinks he is in with the new team and betrays something that cannot be forgiven – he betrays his intelligence. He sets them a riddle based on the conquest of a lion. This is a hinge point in the story. Samson is not just a big strong lad. Now he has demonstrated he has a brain. I imagine they place their drinks down, wipe the froth off their mouths and have him repeat his riddle. They are the dominant culture, the rulers. I get the impression they were further down the pecking order, but they are still Philistines first. This Israelite boy is showing them up.

Since I completed my MPhil degree over ten years ago, I have wanted to write a book like this. I had some powerful allies, Anthony Reddie and Robert Beckford for two (Google them to get a sense of their magnitude in this field of thinking and acting if they are unfamiliar to you). They were supporting and supportive of me developing a black liberative theology for the Church of England. The white area bishop I had at the time, who moved on to higher things, when I mentioned my interest at taking my academic work forward, 'put his drink down, wiped the froth off his mouth', looked me in the eye and said: 'In this [read 'my'] area we don't encourage our curates [the sentence could have finished there] to develop academic pursuits.'

There was a steely look in his eye, as he sought to invoke the obedience I had sworn to him while he had laid his hand on my mini-afro months before. I acquiesced. Enthusiasm dented and naive optimism-shield back to 67 per cent, I approached the church I was sponsored by as curate, a large charismatic church. They specialised in developing a range of programmes and projects to share the story of Christianity. With such a range of resources, I met with the church leader, naive optimism-shield at 82 per cent. He held his mug of coffee, beaming at what brilliant things I had to say. Encouraged by his positive vibe I said to him 'We could develop a diversity course, where the best of everyone's heritage in the church, a very multicultural church, could be taken into account.' 'He put his drink down and wiped the froth off his mouth.' His trademark smile didn't slip, but the meeting was over in a hurry, which is a pity for him, because at that time I did not realise how easy I was making it for him. You see, the diversity course would have been built on race relations, and not on a racial justice model that critiqued whiteness. Kavita Bhanot, in speaking of the publishing industry, says:

The concept of diversity only exists if there is an assumed neutral point from which 'others' are 'diverse'. Putting aside for now the straight, male, middle-classness of that 'neutral' space, its dominant aspect is whiteness ... As writers of colour, we parrot this idea back, reminding white institutions that they need to increase their diversity; appealing to them to let us in, to give some of us a seat at the table too ... Monocultures are bad for business. ... within 20 years the UK BAME population will be 25%. If books don't reflect that, they will become increasingly irrelevant and unprofitable.[2]

So my diversity course would have been a planet orbiting the sun, instead of challenging the sun's primacy. But at that time in my life, the rays of the Delilah church were blinding. With Delilah-style churches, the strategy is shock and awe. You are so dazzled by actually being there that it takes a while to adjust to the light and see what is sniffing around in the shadows. Delilah is used to draw Samson into a trap. To make her money, Delilah had to extract from Samson the source of his mighty strength. It was her job to have him confess his secret. It was long before radioactive gamma rays could bombard a body, or super-solider serums could transform one from zero to hero. No, Samson's power came from a vow his parents made on his behalf, that he was dedicated to God. This vow was expressed through the growing of his hair.

Rastafarians grew their dreadlocks as a protest against the enforced shaved heads of the slaves. As their hair grew, it represented a liberation of their own thoughts – a sacrament of agency and personhood. In the story of Samson his hair acts as a conductor of incredible energy. I imagine him running to do battle and his hair emitting a dull glow as it comes alive, flooding his body with adrenaline and upping his testosterone levels, giving him tremendous power.

Delilah is a victim of the men behind the scenes as much as Samson. She is humiliated by the overlords as Samson teases her with false claims. Eventually his need for her approval outweighs his need to remain vigilant. He gives away his secret of his uncut hair, he submits to her, and is betrayed by her. Samson is sheared and awakens to witness his braids scattered like dead snakes in a pile at his feet. He attempts to activate the change sequence. He snaps out of Delilah's spell, but it is too late to snap out of the fetters. His strength has gone with his hair. He is eventually blinded and bound to the pillars in the Philistine temple of Dagon.

With this type of high-status church, the person of colour becomes a threat to the established order. The system does not exile the person but furnishes them with the illusion that they are being welcomed into the world of the powerful. Delilah appears to be her own person. Being with her gives him the benefits of the group – which he joins but on their terms. He has to lose his power and sacrifice his strength. He is cut off from his people. He is expected to alter his appearance, to assimilate. He becomes blind, not able to see the oppressive system. The warrior becomes a performer and a neutered novelty.

In the church in which I worked, I offered my energy, and the desire to write the diversity course, but I was assigned the 'youth service' and required to dress up and perform in the family services, and entertain the masses. The contents of my brain were not welcome or wanted, and I gave in, lost my strength and paid the cost with my eyes after submitting. I no longer saw racial bias for a long time, as I was too busy singing and dancing for the Dagon worshippers. There is a term my mum would use, a term she'd learned growing up, of someone being degraded to a fool, being a 'papishow', pronounced 'pap-ee-show'. The term may have originated with a mispronunciation of puppet show. You are on the stage, but someone else is pulling the strings. I am like an emptied-out can of coffee, emptied of my contents and story, my lament, my pain, my grief, to be replaced with happy, clappy, flappy, tasty Nescafé coffee, not my fairly traded coffee with its bitter aftertaste coming from bitter experience. Many times I've been reduced to the empty entertainer, a parody of myself. It is a tragic story, as by now Samson cannot both save himself and his people. From the heart of Dagon's temple, leaning on the pillars, his stubby clumps of hair begin to grow. Vengeance and fury trigger an earth-shattering release of strength that breaks the supportive temple pillars. As huge blocks of masonry fall about his head the oppressive system is slowed down and the demolishing temple takes 3,000 adherents with it. When one begins to challenge an established system, it can feel like a one-way ticket, a shunning, a shaming, a silencing, and a sentencing.

Over time, my hair began to grow back in this setting. Although I could not see the whiteness wolves, I could hear them growling. There is such an expectation for clergy in the Church of England to sound a certain way and act a certain way. Although this is exclusionary, it is understandable. The dominant models of leadership are replete with larger than life, posh characters who are enticing, and there is a craving for people to be in with the in-crowd.

I see a number of parallels with Roald Dahl's story *Charlie and the Chocolate Factory*. When I worked for a Delilah-church, it was impenetrable from the outside, and fairly inscrutable on the inside. It was like Willy Wonka's Chocolate Factory. The church I was part of promised its clergy a top spot directing global affairs. The hope of being part of a world-changing vision, of bringing chocolate to the masses! A number of us were chosen to be in close proximity to Willy Wonka himself! We had our notebooks at the ready, we would pick up all he was dropping. In *Charlie and the Chocolate Factory*, Charlie Bucket is blinded by the brilliance of Willy Wonka and all that Willy produces. Charlie's desire to break out of his humble, poor moorings almost sends the family into further difficulties. The family use their hard-earned savings to buy him chocolate, instead of pooling their resources and building a local economy. There is an underlying judgement made that Charlie's situation is bleak, it is in deficit, and that is the way of the world. The collective power of his family unit is disregarded. The ways in which they are resilient are ignored. The intergenerational mutual investment is obscured. The way in which Charlie is unconditionally loved and affirmed is remarkable but minimised. In fact, Willy Wonka himself gets rid of his staff from the factory, contributing to Charlie's poverty. However, the larger systemic issues are never in view, whereas the factory with its hallucinogenic qualities is a marvel and the prime focus. The factory with the wonderland of rooms where one is taught how to make a product more addictive, more marketable, is seen as the place to be. Willy Wonka's competition to search for the golden ticket becomes like the game show *The Apprentice*, where the winner takes all. The idolatry of the man and the product is unashamedly portrayed and the ruthless individualism which is triggered among the final contestants is lauded. The chosen few are in awe of Willy Wonka, the benign dictator who allows the disobedient and dissenting children to perish in his machinery. There are significant reasons why a Charlie Bucket would be helpful as Willy Wonka's heir. It is like Willy Wonka love-bombing Charlie, then becoming inconsistent once he is ensconced.

Charlie is ultimately chosen because he has least power and is most manipulable. He can run the factory because he will run it as Wonka wants. The key factor in Charlie over the others is his suggestibility, his unquestioning obedience to Willy Wonka. Also he has a grandparent, not a parent, with him, so he is more vulnerable and the grandparent is just as enamoured and uncritical. It also means there is more room for Willy Wonka to assume the father-figure role uncontested. The church I used to work for had three key values: loyalty, hard work and love, primarily on behalf of our very own Willy Wonka who really was the king in that setting, and emperor of a larger domain.

But Charlie is a white boy, so how does this apply to people of colour? Well, actually, Charlie was black! Roald Dahl originally wanted Charlie to be a negro boy. But he was persuaded by his agent not to do it, among a number of changes.[3] So black Charlie was revised. But that older story demonstrates how some people of colour in the Church of England are treated in comparison with their white counterparts.

In the original story, black Charlie arrives at the factory, and he is wide-eyed and loyal. It is more of a detective story and Charlie has a natural curiosity. He comes apart from the main group and finds a fascinating room called the Easter Room.[4] This room contains a whole host of moulds designed for various

Easter products, chick moulds, bunny moulds, and child-size moulds. Charlie investigates the child mould. He backs into it, discovering it is his size. Horrifically his stepping into it triggers the chocolate release mechanism and he is covered in chocolate. It hardens on him and he is stuck in place,

> as still as a statue inside his thick hard suit of chocolate.[5]

This is the moment that Charlie is objectified. The story goes on that Willy Wonka returns to the room, and seeing this chocolate child-sized Easter egg, takes it home to show his family. Yes, in this version Willy isn't single, he has a son called Freddie, but is still strange. Charlie is taken to Willy Wonka's house as a trophy and becomes his possession. Charlie is trapped within the mould and lacks agency to break free. Fryer speaks of black servants in the houses of wealthy whites, saying:

> black servants conferred on their masters and mistresses an air of luxurious well-being. They were at once charming, exotic ornaments, objects of curiosity, talking points, and above all symbols of prestige ...[6]

Black Charlie foils a robbery

Meanwhile in Willy Wonka's house, Charlie is locked in place as a trophy for his family. One imagines Willy's son salivating, awaiting the moment to consume his prize. All is quiet in the house – the family are asleep. From his chocolate jail, black Charlie witnesses a group of thieves break in. His love for Willy leads to an effort that results in liberation in order to help apprehend the criminals. He is free – to a degree – of the mould, of the caricature, of the stereotype. But he is still in Willy's house. He is now subject to another form of slavery.

> after the dark horrors of that box ... to Charlie Bucket, it seemed as though he had literally come back to life from the dead.[7]

Is Willy so pleased that he celebrates Charlie and lets him have his factory? No, in this version it is not Charlie but *black* Charlie, and black Charlie does not get the empire, he is allowed to run a shop stocked with Willy Wonka's products.

In the church I worked for, it was strongly indicated to me, in a number of ways, that my class and racial bracket was 'wrong'. I could, however, have a little church stocked with Willy Wonka's products. In time I realised that all my loyalty, love, and hard work would not be rewarded. I was stuck in a mould from which I could not easily escape.

The book of Esther in the Hebrew Scriptures resonates with the Charlie story. The story is set in a period of the Persian empire. There is a powerful emperor known as 'the king of kings'. His name is Xerxes. He is like a playboy billionaire. He holds a huge party to display his opulence among the good and the great of his vast domain. He wants to show he is in charge at home too, so he summons his attractive wife Vashti. He wants her to parade for his male friends. They can look at, but not touch, his property. This is demeaning and degrading. Vashti is beautiful and brave, and she says no to the king of kings. This is not the done thing and her act of resistance threatens the status quo. Xerxes' advisors are afraid she will become an icon and it would lead to a blight of equal marriages and instant feminism breaking out all over the kingdom. Vashti is exiled.

The white, upper-middle class, priests/bishops – usually male – have to work very hard not to pedestal their current rare gems of black and brown clergy. The times myself and other clergy of colour have felt like exotic accessories of our so-called betters are multiple. There is the fear that if we do not perform the emotional labour needed to keep smiling, we will be cut off – cut out of our slice of the pie. But sometimes for your integrity's sake you have to say 'no', even if that means you have to go. For Vashti, it may have been the only power she had. If you're not safe, if the boat is overfull and the water is coming in, you may be pushed out, but hopefully you can swim to safety before the whole ship sinks and the sharks catch the scent.

Esther is an Israelite woman and part of the dominated

people group. She has a different strategy to Vashti. She finds herself in a 'Persia's next top model' style contest. Xerxes is looking for a replacement. Esther can pass as a native. She wins the contest and the prize is marriage to Xerxes. Unlike Samson she keeps a link to home. Although she largely hides the extent and scope of her heritage, she has something of a hinterland in Mordecai, her uncle, who secretly advises her. You cannot take on the system on your own. You need some backup in high places to help guide you through. One needs connection to community to provide perspective and purpose.

Mordecai represents the older generation. Historically he has proved his worth. Like black Charlie, he has foiled a crime. Mordecai discovered a plot to harm Xerxes and his actions prevented it. Mordecai now has immunity, and has status with both the court and his hidden community. Younger clergy of colour need the older generations to be our elders, to uphold us, and guide our steps in what can be threatening and dangerous environments.

Esther receives intelligence of a plan endorsed by the king of kings to enact genocide on her ethnic group. At this stage he is unaware of her ethnic origins. He did not ask the ubiquitous question black and brown people suffer, which is: 'Where are you from?' Esther and Mordecai team up and, through Esther, Xerxes is convinced of the need for her people to be safe. He replies that his orders cannot be undone, and that the kill team is in place and will be carrying out his orders. However, he writes another order which instructs that her people can fight back.

If you are a person of colour in the Church of England, and doing well, and you have a hinterland, is this your time to both convert the king of kings and expel the rot? Could English priests and bishops still encased in the whiteness (Club) lose the whiteness husk and liberate the true potential of a noble and enabling English identity? Can they step out and aside from their whiteness backdrop, divesting themselves of power, permitting those in the kingdom to fight back? For the Church of England, the mistakes made back in 1985 cannot be revisited, but can the current leadership encourage people of colour to fight against the mistakes made all that time ago? How can people of the present be empowered to undo the wrongs of the past, without present obstruction, even if it means destruction of the (Club)?

The will to survive is a powerful impulse. Will Jadis happily retire, riding her whiteness elephant, her wolves dragging their tails behind them? Can the little band of people of colour in the Church of England create a stir, cause some holy devastation, or are we mere decoration? A token gesture?

Notes

1 BraveSlave, Vol. One, 2018.

2 Bhanot, K. (2020), *Decolonise, not Diversify*, Media Diversified. Available online at: https://mediadiversified.org/2015/12/30/is-diversity-is-only-for-white-people/.

3 Sturrock, Donald (2010), *Storyteller*, New York: Simon and Schuster, p. 398.

4 www.nytimes.com/2017/09/22/books/review/roald-dahl-black-charlie-chocolate-factory.html. I am very happy that when I emailed the researcher Catherine Keyser she was incredibly helpful in giving me so much useful background on this hidden history.

5 Keyser, Catherine (2017), *Candy Boys and Chocolate Factories: Roald Dahl, Racialization, and Global Industry*, MFS Modern Fiction Studies, Vol. 63, no. 3, pp. 403–28. Project MUSE, p. 404.

6 Fryer, P. (1984), *Staying Power: The History of Black People in Britain*, London: Pluto Press, p. 73.

7 Keyser, *Candy*, p. 404.

9

Token Gesture

In the writing of this book I have encountered giants who have put their shoulders to the boulder of racism that blocks the light for so many. But as I look over the last generation it feels in many ways as if we are condemned like Sisyphus. Sisyphus is cursed with the futile act of rolling a boulder to the top of the hill only to witness it roll back down, before having to fetch it once more and repeat the action for all of time.

Bishop Rose was right: 'We don't have the numbers.' Others said the same to me. I wanted to believe that if enough of us tore up the old scripts, if we applied more strength and had a clearer strategy, we could turn the needle. But reading about tokenism in the workplace with Rosabeth Moss Kanter, I learned a technical definition of 'minority' and people of colour in the Church of England are a long way from this. The percentage to justify calling ourselves a minority is 35 per cent. Her categories are as follows.

Uniform

The ratio here is 100%:0%. The group is all of one type. Before I arrived in my parish in Suburbia, the local parishes, the ecumenical presence, and the wider group of Church of England churches referred to as the deanery, were all white. Despite differing church traditions, whiteness was a common denominator. There had never been a black priest in operation there before. Some would challenge my apparent gripe with 'If you wanted not to be a token, why go to a white area?' Well, my conviction had been that the true church is universal, and its priests and ministers should be able to flourish in any setting. The culture and institutions may have an elite white operating system at play, but the true church should be free from cultural chains to bring the best of the world into any part of the world: a vision of everyone, from everywhere, impacting everybody. The church should be – could be – a portal to another world where the principles of justice, the person of Jesus, and the philosophy of journey prevails. But it is not.

Moss Kanter states how, in this stage of an organisation,

> members and observers may never become self-conscious about the common dominant culture and type, which remains taken for granted and implicit. But the presence of a person or two bearing a different set of social characteristics increases the self-consciousness of the numerically dominant population and the consciousness of observers about what makes the dominants a class. They become more aware both of their commonalities and their difference from the token, and to preserve their commonality, they try to keep the token slightly outside, to offer a boundary for the dominants.[1]

The social capital and social cohesion happen in a way that excludes rather than includes. I was invited to attend a clergy cricket match, with clergy drawn from across the city. The team, dressed in brilliant cricket whites, were all white, captained by one of our white bishops, and I felt that a curtain had been drawn back. I had never combined that set of men before. The team were comprised of men who held differing theological standpoints, on sexuality, say, or remarriage after divorce, or men who would express their worship in completely different ways, whether hands raised in wild abandon or knees bent before the altar. The team also included men who would preach for thirty minutes from the Bible with a clear answer and others who would preach for ten minutes using a piece of art to inspire a question. Yet on that sunny day in Suburbia the majority of their backgrounds, their access to particular forms of education, their connections provided by parents and grandparents – all of this had bonded them. The shared kinship was the baseline unity. Ideological differences or worship preferences were of a secondary order. And this is where the business took place. At a church dedication service one of the team shared publicly 'the idea for this began on a cricket pitch', and we all laughed.

Skewed (Token)

The ratio is 85%:15%. My arrival in Suburbia changed the dynamics, without me doing anything, just by simply looking like a person of colour, whether or not I even felt like one. As a Church of England priest, I cannot be inconspicuous. I cannot blend in without pressure to be on display. I don't have the option of invisibility in the many contexts in which I find myself. In many churches I take a seat and by simply showing up I am conspicuous. I sit around a trustee board meeting and I am conspicuous. I show up at an event as the one black member among sometimes one or two hundred white people – often well-to-do people at that – and the class dynamic is activated too. Imagine a kitchen. On the surface near the sink rests a fruit bowl full of plump, juicy oranges. In your mind's eye picture someone placing a bright green Granny Smith, freshly picked from the orchard, in the centre of the display. What is your eye drawn to? Which fruit will be devoured first? Moss Kanter says:

> Tokens are more easily stereotyped than people found in greater proportion. If there were enough people of the token's type to let discrepant examples occur, it is eventually possible that the generalisation would change to accommodate the accumulated cases ... It is also easier for tokens to find an instant identity by conforming to the preexisting stereotypes.[2]

Tilted

The ratio is 65%:35%. The following is from Moss Kanter again. Here is the tipping point for change:

> [A]s the group moves from skewed to tilted, tokens turn into a less individually noticed minority. But for tokens, there is a 'law of increasing returns': as individuals of their type represent a smaller numerical proportion of the over-all group, they each potentially capture a larger share of the awareness given to that group.[3]

She also describes how it is at this point that the dominant group shifts into being the majority group, and the other group can call itself the minority. It is at the point where there is 35% and more. Before that point, the tokens are symbols, not individuals. This is the point at which coalitions can be built.

The Church of England BAME contingent of clergy is less than 5%, although the number of those in training is increasing. If you find yourself a token, it seems easier to attempt to blend in and claim a colour blindness or even try to adopt whiteness as a person of colour. Or if not the clergy person of colour, perhaps those close to them.

'I want to be white and live in a white family.'[4]

This line is from a speech by Wilfred Wood to Synod in 1988. He was recounting a discussion he had with his six-year-old daughter. He went on to describe how a societal negative perception of blackness inhibits black participation and makes blackness an insecure foundation upon which to build a life. That was back in 1988. Things have moved on, different ethnic groups are doing better now according to our Archbishop of Canterbury in *Reimagining Britain*. But I had an experience during my time in Suburbia which demonstrated that what Wilfred as a black clergyman experienced back then has

contemporary relevance over 30 years later. This poem arose
in response to an experience of one of my children.

I'm Ugly

Last night, I stood by my child, by their bed,
Through warm tears, they looked at me, and said:

'I'm ugly, Daddy.'

Where had they swallowed these lies?
I felt small, grief-stricken, less than half my size.

They went on to share that their classmate
spouted hate, when they said:

'White people are f-ing better than *"the"* blacks.'
'the' as in *o-the-r.*

How can I at the altar preside?
When it is my body and blood
which are broken?
Can I persuade local white allies, to rally to our cause
Or am I simply a token?

How can I address this? Should I just suppress this?
Is the area afraid of diversity, whilst I am afraid of
    adversity?
Sure I've got a lovely vicarage,
my own little slice of white privilege.

Why would I threaten that
and disturb the status quo?
Some might say I'm a house negro,
who is complicit,
in my child's explicit
exposure to the invisible beast,

leaving them believing they are the least
whilst I process as a smiling priest.

BraveSlave[5]

It is heartbreaking to consider not just a clergy person of colour in the midst of a struggle but, should they have brought children with them into a new area, a whole new layer of pain seeing their child so distressed over their ethnicity and the negative association they are forming. All children respond differently and my other children seemed unaffected by being the token brown children. However, my sensitive child holds a concentrated form of what we as a family have experienced and which the wider community can seem oblivious to. All priests of whatever background should be able to flourish in any setting with the right resources and relationships. In the instance documented above, white friends did what they could to support us as a family, and I am grateful for their offers of solidarity. However, as there are so few clergy of colour the argument for an overhaul of the system to insulate other clergy of colour and their families if they have them remains unheard.

'Until the Church of England cleans up its act should we be putting minority ethnic Anglicans through this appalling situation?'[6]

The question is from Glynne Gordon-Carter as she received complaint after complaint from people of colour in the Church of England while she was in her role in CMEAC. The question haunts me. Why do we continue to expose people to psychologically damaging situations? The ship that is already overfull and unable to care for its current passengers is not fit for purpose. There is such a push for integration but at what point do we say 'enough is enough'?

The pressure on clergy of colour who are born and raised here to integrate their English upbringings with their heritages and histories can be a complex and fraught task – a liminality of belonging to no one and being nowhere is a high possibility. Professor of Sociology Andrew Pilkington speaks of an 'imperialism–racism view'. He describes it as giving those who are white a higher place in the pecking order in English society. He says that White South Africans, Kiwis, White Australians and White Americans have been woven into the fabric of English society with less upheaval and challenge.[7]

In the Church of England, people of colour are referred to as the minority. We press on tirelessly agitating for change, but according to Moss Kanter our classifications are wrong. Using terms like Black and Minority Ethnic and CMEAC are too optimistic. These terms assume a majority ethnicity that acts as a benign neutral backdrop with which others can assimilate, and to which they can relate. According to Moss Kanter, people of colour are not a minority. We are tokens, and that reveals that the white English assumptions are not a benign neutrality, but a harmful dominant society. CMEAC is called a Committee for Minority Ethnic Concerns. It could be called CTEC or the Committee for Token Ethnic Concerns. Is being a token gesture enough of an incentive to stay?

An example of what tokenism can feel like in the Church of England

I sat on a high-ranking bishop's advisory panel to select a new bishop for one of the episcopal areas of his diocese. It was an honour to be considered. I felt a frisson of excitement. I was to be part of the production of the system, not simply the promotion of the system. We all sat down around a table on the upper floor of a grand house. I had not initially realised I was the only person of colour there, as I felt it such an honour to be among Christian colleagues. Ethnicity was not a conscious concern. I was at the table and in the room where decisions were made. It did not take me long to realise how wrong I was.

One of the senior figures took the role of introducing each of us. When he came to me he said 'He is here to represent BAME, and younger clergy.' I looked at the notes we'd been given and sure enough I had missed that description which had come after my name. They were getting two for one, apparent youth and ethnicity. The cards are so stacked that the BAME card is often the only currency one has. I felt this to be a limiting and a narrowing of who I was in their eyes. Their understanding of my blackness is a flimsy cardboard cut-out of the real embodied reality. Now that I knew I was there to represent my race, surely my job was done. What if we could have read the mind of this senior figure as he introduced some of the other attendees as well as myself? It might have sounded like this:

This is Fr Roderick Montague-Smythe. He is here as a well-to-do white English man. He is also here to represent the interests of very, very old Etonians. We are humbled he has descended to us from such a lofty perch, in the upper echelons of rarefied society to briefly allow us a fleeting glimpse of his magnificence. And I can personally attest to the quality of his golf. He and I regularly battle for the club trophy. Anyway, this is my BAME colleague. Erm, who is of dusky complexion and smiley face. He is here to watch how it all happens. Like a nervous intern, he will be overawed and underused. He will speak when spoken to and go forth from here singing our praises because all black people are great singers. [Not true.]

Over the times we met I found it interesting to learn about the process of selecting a bishop. I increasingly found my role and opinion being managed; there was a subtle sidelining imperceptible to all but the trained eye or ear. On interview day, myself, the woman's representative and the youth representative were situated downstairs as far away from the action as possible. We learned we were not there as interviewers, but as people to give the candidates a view of our various areas of expertise. The youth specialist was skilled with teenagers, so she came with a body of knowledge. For myself and the female priest, we just came with our bodies. A female body and a black body were our birth traits that relegated us downstairs. We were not there to ask questions of the interviewees, but to provide answers – a silencing, the way of the cross. The real work was done by the white men upstairs, whose birth traits placed them in the position of Crown and honoured members of the (Club).

Is it any wonder why some white spaces feel so unsafe for me? How do I become so self-conscious that I am unable to offer anything of value and instead follow the script I imagine the people around the table want to hear? I can feel as if I am forcing myself into a space not designed for me. The nuances and the subtleties, the unspoken rules, are like a set of trip-wires that I stumble over on my way to the table. Some call it the white gaze, how I perceive and sometimes know others are looking at me. Women may relate to the male gaze, those who are LGBTQI+ may know the cis gender heterosexual gaze, those with disabilities may know the gaze of the able-bodied. It is a moment of conspicuousness where one aspect of your character is hardened into all you are understood to be. I remember visiting someone in a residential home for the elderly. As I passed an open door, a white elderly woman was sat on her bed. As we passed her open door I looked in from the corridor and smiled and waved at her. She recoiled in horror and thundered:

'Get away you darky thug!'

I was frightened by the explosion. She was afraid of who she thought me to be. I was with others on this visit and none of us referred to the incident. That was an extreme vocalised fear. Her mind may not have been strong but her voice was and it lingers in my memory. The white gaze predetermines who and what is being looked at, based on conjecture, caricature and conditioning. It is an unspoken objectification, where white-ness is the norm and the positive depiction of humanity and reality. Part of the problem is that if you've been subjected to the white gaze for long enough, the internalisation can lead to a hardening and an expectation and you have to work hard not to perform to type. You begin to act in a way you are expected to, instead of behaving in the way you've elected to. A number of disrespected black clergy colleagues have expressed dissatis-faction at their white colleagues pulling rank. No matter how *we* feel about ourselves, others have another version of 'us' to replace the real 'us' with. George Yancy uses a Jean-Paul Sartre quote to demonstrate this:

> For three thousand years, the white man has enjoyed the privilege of seeing without being seen ... the light from his eyes drew each thing out of the shadow of its birth.[8]

The exposure arising from a sense of that relegation and negation by white society can lead to a protecting of oneself. Stephen Pattison's book explores the effect and impact of shame. Pattison speaks of a 'chronic' shame that is:

> Internalised as part of the personality by individuals and groups who endure lasting oppression ... [they] seem to gain a sense of passivity, inferiority and non-personhood ... the state of shamed non-personhood seems in part a survival strategy that allows conformity and a certain amount of invisibility.[9]

Pattison also avers a chronic shame characteristic as that of 'adopting the oppressor's point of view. They often see themselves with contempt.'[10]

What is the version of limited blackness I am battling to overthrow? Does it arise from an English fear of a black ruling class? We need a bigger, better boat, adapted for wheelchairs, with toilets for all, with paintings and icons of all the heroes. But there is such a failure of imagination to conceptualise the trapped token person of colour teaching or leading the dominant group. There is a fear of black and brown people holding power over white people. It may help to consider this issue in the context of our battlefields.

The danger of Trading Places

Re-Member-ing

In the world's war
bodies charcoal and ashen alike,
stood side by side,
against the enemy,
in the furnace of conflict.

Mere boys taught how to
hate in Khaki hid.
All equally
oppressed,
pressured,
persuaded,
government aided,
captured,
to fight for freedom.

Those who conscientiously objected
were abjected
to prison and given,
a dressing down,
as lady truth was dressed up,
and sold on to the
poor masses
as an easy conquest.

The white poor finding pride
as the bunting flapped and
tea cups clinked a fanfare celebrating
their rite of passage,
in becoming men,
in becoming sacrifices,
fodder to bullets
and shells,
and those who would return
would be shells,

and some would never grow beyond
the tangled, and terrible trauma,
which
lurked and lurched in the fragile locked boxes of their minds.
The public hero hallowed, in time,
became the private hollow harrowed.
The proud British Empire converted
its slaves into subjects,
and its subjects into soldiers,
its most able men were recruited and
taught to use the very weapons that once subjected
them on islands and lands, that were no longer theirs.

'The mother country accepts all bastard sons
as long as they can
carry guns.'

Now those subjects would fire at white
Europeans who were never their master.

In the world's war bodies
charcoal and ashen alike
lay side by side against the
futility of the furnace of conflict.

Body parts blanketed with crimson speak of war's
indiscriminate thirst for blood,
As soldiers limbs lay in torn ground and raped earth,
the cadavers no longer have enemies,
as the parts lay alongside the other victims from the
other side,
they make up a composite humanity with what remains.
The lifeless bodies a silent prophecy, never to be heard.

Until we can re-member our body parts, and remember
we are a part of a larger whole, we are hollow and harrowed.

Can we see ourselves through the other's eyes,
our shared frailty and our mutual bond?
Can we lay down our mechanical arms,
and extend our true arms to embrace?
Then we may find ourselves held by the one with holes in
hands and side.
As new men and women we stand from bruised ground
our scars
a birthmark of the new age to come,
shielded in the shadow of the one who called down
forgiveness
on his fear bound executioners,
the cosmic force of uncoercive love,
who is always amongst us,
whispering through tears the word 'peace'.

BraveSlave[11]

The British Empire was the largest empire in the world with
400,000,000 subjects and covering over a quarter of the earth's
landmass.[12] The sense of dominance and superiority was seemingly unquestioned and uncontested. By 1914 the anxiety about
black leadership rose in the theatre of war. The South African
Native Congress, which would lead to the African National
Congress, hoped support for the war effort would lead to a
greater sense of autonomy as recognition of a demonstration
of loyalty in England's time of need.[13] There was a problem
with the involvement of black troops. Olusoga puts it like this:

It was a phenomenon that challenged the central tenets of
colonial theory ... In the war in Europe, black and brown
men were ordered to fight and kill white men. All the colonial
powers worried that once armed, and once shown that the
myth of white supremacy was just that, soldiers from Africa
and Asia would prove the greatest threat to the long-term
futures of their empires ...

This is not to be underestimated. The power given over to black and brown men, to have power over the lives of white men – even the enemy troops – was a deeper fear reflected through the church. White American bishops determined to superficially show catholicity and did not want ethnic differences to be the focus of their carefully worded statements. I include quotes from two American Episcopalian bishops that show this. The first is by Bishop Alfred M. Randolph of Virginia in a speech made to the Diocesan Council:

> The government of a church by the people is the highest mission of the world to which the people can be called ... involves a strain upon intelligence, upon moral principle and upon all the elements of character which result from the highest discipline of Christian civilization ... the question, with reference to the Negro as a legislator in the Episcopal Church, is not a question of race, a question of color, but it is a question of faculty, of ability. It is a question of capacity of character.[14]

So we see the implicit message; white priests are seen to have a greater ability to think, and have the stamina to endure the pressure. I am coming to a realisation that I have picked up this weapon and turned the barrel of the gun on myself. Let me take us to a plainly decorated conference room in Church House, the primary home for the affairs of the diocese I served for a decade. I am sitting discussing my hopes for a new clergy move with my area bishop, the one I was involved in appointing, and an archdeacon. They sit and listen as I hear myself say:

> I want to learn the breadth of the Anglican church and have someone teach me, help me grasp the catholic side of faith. So I can become more confident with liturgy and administering communion, with someone who can be a mentor to me.

The solution was found for me to be an associate priest, with a priest in the neighbouring parish offering me the help I needed to lead in this tradition of church. The sense of humble inferiority I articulated I had thought was all my own. And it was a laudable, commendable desire but I need not have talked myself down, volunteering a subservient position. My second quote is the words of a white bishop from Georgia, in the deep south; in 1916 Bishop Frederick Reese addressed black clergymen by saying:

> I do not believe that our colored people as a race are yet prepared to minister in an ecclesiastical organization without the cooperation and assistance of their white brethren. Are you people ready to cut loose entirely from the white people, people in government, education, social betterment, and in the church, and face the whole tremendous problem of human life without any reliance on the white man? Would you do it if you could? I do not say this to disparage you. God knows, I would not do this ... You may remember indeed that Anglo-Saxon churchmen have earned by centuries of toil and suffering the right to leadership in teaching and guarding the faith and order of the church.[15]

My conversation with the bishop and archdeacon was using Bishop Frederick Reese's script, which I had somehow learned. I thought myself ill-equipped to lead. In my interview for Suburbia, I made it clear I was happy with the role of Associate and seemed unsure about whether or not I would be right to be in sole charge. In part, this is because I doubted the confidence others would have had in me to lead. Yet I was doing a decent enough job according to most people I knew and could well have pursued the role of vicar of the parish. Indeed, in time I attempted to create the conditions to enable my promotion, but it was the wrong time for a church transitioning towards a new direction of travel. Nevertheless the words of Reese from over 100 years ago were coded into my thinking. Was I willing to cut off my reliance on the white man? Was it tantamount to sawing off the branch I was perched on, which was connected to the true tree? What would enable me to find the courage within myself to lead beyond myself? What would it take for the community around me to hold me in equal esteem to my white colleagues? We only have to look at the paucity of black and brown bishops to think about tokenism. But could Olusoga's perspective shed some light on why people of colour are conditioned to believe they cannot hold power? White superiority and its adherents are afraid of subservience to former subjects.

There was also a concerted effort by the good people of the Association of Black Clergy to influence the challenge of a lack of black and brown bishops. During my conversation with Tunde Roberts, he told me:

Tunde   What we did was to write to Downing Street and say 'Look, we would like to be meeting with you twice a year because of under-representation. Downing Street has the Crown Appointments Commission, and the Lord Chancellor also has some responsibility. So I would have lists of our members sent to Downing Street. Members who we believed were right for senior leadership positions, and those who showed promise. The government were good to us, they would give us an appointment twice a year and we would go to meet them there.

Me   So you compiled your own preferment lists?

Tunde   Yes, we met them twice a year. It was helpful sharing our ideas. But there is a limit to what the government could do. The bishops tended to appoint who they wanted. The government official would say this particular bishop does what they want to do regardless of our recommendations. But we thought it was a good way of the government knowing about our candidates, so they could promote them too.

But all this optimism and great effort expended resulted in very little. We have had over 30 years of a concerted and determined message to those who have power in the Church of England. We have requested that they do all they can to represent and include all of England, and all former subjects that once fell under the empire. But we are token gestures. Earlier in this chapter, I talked about my child saying 'I am ugly' as they compared themselves to their white peers, receiving explicit and implicit messaging that they were deemed inferior. We as a family gathered round to nurture and foster their self-esteem, friends also gathered round to encourage us and our child, yet other institutions to which they belonged saw it as the child's problem to deal with and the task as raising resilience in the child rather than lowering prejudice in the institution. A powerful figure in the story of the early church was Paul of Tarsus. He began a church in Corinth and in one of his letters to them he said the following:

> The way God designed our bodies is a model for understanding our lives together as a church: every part dependent on every other part, the parts we mention and the parts we don't, the parts we see and the parts we don't. If one part hurts, every other part is involved in the hurt, and in the healing. If one part flourishes, every other part enters into the exuberance. (1 Cor. 12.25–26)

But the fear of a loss of power and status and the certainty of white superiority lead to an all-out wipeout of the least of these, an attack on the parts in pain unaware that we are all part of a larger whole. Until the token is regarded, the whole church will remain broken and will eventually be discarded. There are those the Church of England distorts through exclusion, and others who feel forced to contort in collusion. True answers are rarely sought; now the conclusions.

Notes

1 Moss Kanter, Rosabeth (1977), *Men and Women of the Corporation*, New York: BasicBooks.

2 Ibid., ebook location 4470.

3 Ibid., 4457.

4 Wood, Wilfred (1994), *Keep the Faith Baby*, Oxford: The Bible Reading Fellowship.

5 Unpublished collection of poems.

6 Gordon-Carter, Glynne, *An Amazing Journey*, p. 91.

7 Pilkington, A. (2003), *Racial Disadvantage and Ethnic Diversity in Britain*, Basingstoke: Palgrave Macmillan, p. 41.

8 Yancy, G. (2016), *Black Bodies, White Gazes: The continuing significance of race in America*, London: Rowman and Littlefield International, p. 8.

9 Pattison, S. (2000), *Shame, Theory, Theology, and Therapy*, Cambridge: Cambridge University Press, p. 134.

10 Ibid., p. 105.

11 Unpublished collection of poems.

12 Olusoga, David (2014), *The World's War*, London: Head of Zeus, p. 18.

13 Ibid., p. 21.

14 Lewis, H. (1996), *Yet With a Steady Beat*, Pennsylvania: Trinity Press International, p. 69.

15 Ibid., p. 200.

Conclusions?

Ethnic minority people are consistently under-represented among the clergy. Ethnic minority people are also under-represented in lay roles of responsibility in comparison of their numbers on electoral rolls.[1]

Another finding demonstrates that proportionately 'Black and Black British adults have been found to be more likely to belong to Church of England local congregations than their white counterparts.'[2] But we are tokens. There is not a sufficient pool from which one of us could truly trade places within the current system.

What would a British born and raised black person need in place to one day become Archbishop of Canterbury?

I am not a Black British-born person, so I can only speak from my own perspective. I realise that as one born outside Britain, I seem to be afforded more opportunities than my British-born BAME sisters and brothers. Our church needs to recognise, celebrate, and enable the voice and experience of this particular constituency to be heard and to actively shape its life. We need to be honest in naming the gap. We need to be intentional in setting a pathway to representation and participation through measurable outcomes.

The ability to see themselves reflected in senior leadership as the norm rather than the exception, and of course the call of God to serve in that capacity.

To be Oxbridge educated. And very charismatic.

Black people like myself need to not only be invited to eat at the table, but we need to be asked to speak, and to have our voices heard. Many of us are calling – within the institution – for racial justice. For racial shalom. As it stands, the Church of England is far from a place of racial shalom. In fact, I would say that it isn't even serious about aiming at racial shalom.

That their voices are heard and heeded even when it is the voice of lament; when we demand for things to change, at the expense of centuries of white legacy. When we feel free to say – in whatever ecclesial circles – what we really think, to people who are receptive and not using institutional power to quiet us, then I would say that the conversation has truly begun. The Church of England has been alluded to by Liberation Theologian Paulo Friere as 'anti-prophetic' because it has a distaste for the voice of challenge. The day it gets a taste for the prophetic black voice is the day I am happy to see a Black, British AB of C. Until then, I cannot see there being anyone in such a position who could speak for me, or my experience. It's not enough just to have a black face. We need a black voice too. (Maybe with a bit of bass in it.)

Very thick skin and robustness. There would need to be some re-education at parish level for local clergy to understand something of equality and barriers.

Be on the preferential list; a BAME Prime Minister; few more Archdeacons, Deans, Theological College Principals perhaps?

Structural changes which entrench equality, competence and recognise the need to be inclusive. Tall order perhaps.

A lot of changed hearts, a lot of courage, superhuman thick skin and clear unwavering sense of calling.

Has that person even been born yet? Are the conditions right yet? Will an Archbishop Michael or Archbishop Michelle Curry be possible on English soil anytime soon? Does the Church of England offer black and brown people in its cathedrals, communities, churches and colleges anything of relevance for their whole lives?

A generation ago I was swinging my legs, eating popcorn, watching the movie *Trading Places*. It seemed anything was possible. A generation ago, we had the *Faith in the City* report, followed by repeated attempts for affirmative action with a plan and a plea for more brown and black people in General Synod. We had celebrations of our black and brown heritages which we used in part to prove our English credentials. We joined hands with others across the pond and beyond. Yet it was never enough, never long-lasting.

Space does not permit me to describe the failed attempts to reform theological education by adding provision for post-colonial perspectives and liberation theologies using fresh and dynamic learning strategies and drawing on multiple cultures. I am grateful for the many people who told me their stories of places like the Simon of Cyrene College supported by the Southwark diocese, and all that it hoped to achieve before it was abandoned, or the project in the London diocese that John Sentamu pushed forward which again was under-resourced and relegated to the scrap heap. A generation ago we had the Association of Black Clergy, and all they did to attempt to be a pressure group to storm the citadel, and to offer protection to those battered by racist thoughts, words and deeds. They worked effectively with the press, the government and equalities organisations to hold the church to account, yet they ultimately failed and split into factions. When you are unable to defeat the enemy without, you relocate that enemy within. We even had a huge attempt to have the Lambeth Conference relocated to South Africa to demonstrate that we were the global church. Shiny mega-churches seek to save the Church of England by creating black Charlies as diversity display trophies and tokens. Some bishops pull away from the whiff of pain they pick up in the people of colour that they encounter.

I asked the question if we needed a Truth and Reparations Commission within the Church of England when we considered Bishop Such and Such in the chapter entitled 'No Pain Allowed'. This Commission could be a sharing of stories followed by recompense, and maybe relationship. But perhaps Truth and Reconciliation is enough? A sharing of stories followed by relationship, and maybe recompense. But what would that relationship be based on? Some would argue that a version of what happened in South Africa would be a huge step forward and should be pursued. If we reminded ourselves that after the end of institutionalised apartheid Nelson Mandela appointed Desmond Tutu as chair of the Truth and Reconciliation Commission, the TRC. It was a desire to bring together the rainbow nation, and avoid bloodshed and a form of civil conflict. There was an opportunity to hear the pain many suffered under the systemic oppression, and then a hoped-for healing of the pain through forgiveness, and moving on. Tutu's approach was monumentally ambitious and almost universally lauded as he evoked the concept of *Ubuntu*. One definition of the word is 'being a person through other people' and another is 'I am because we are'. The Truth and Reconciliation Commission sought to broker a compromise between a number of white apartheid leaders who wanted amnesty, and those of the African National Congress who wanted to prosecute those who perpetrated the crimes against humanity.[3]

There could be a temptation among some of my readers now to ask me and other people of colour to recount our past pains in order to hear for yourself, and to your satisfaction that there is a case to be made. Then there may be a desire for us all to move away from these painful episodes. The TRC interim report said:

We open wounds only in order to cleanse them, to deal with the past effectively and so to close the door on that dark and horrendous past forever ...[4]

That seems to make sense. Tutu in the final report said that we shut the door on the past... so that we could move into the glorious future of a new kind of society ...

A society where Jadis is no more in control. The howling wolves are howling with laughter and camaraderie with all, not howling with hunger searching for the next target. In the Hebrew Scriptures, in the prophetic book of Isaiah, we read a type of fable that points to the desired outcome of the South African TRC. We have a fleeting glimpse of what many, many people over a number of years have been hoping would happen in the Church of England generally and the Cross and the Crown (Club) in particular. We shall see our cathedrals, our colleges, our congregations, and our communities transformed when

> The wolf will live with the lamb, the leopard will lie down with the goat, the calf and the lion and the yearling together; and a little child will lead them.[5]

The wolf and the lamb in harmony. This is an alternative vision of prey and predator. In fact, those categories are annihilated. The two are living, working and flourishing together, and that is true community, a combination of a Kenyan safari park and an English farm, where animals who are predators play with animals that are usually their prey. In this version of the world, Jadis' wolves have changed their diet. The little child is leading them. The suffering Christ who has gone the way of the cross is able to bring them together and lead them out as equals and companions.

In Ben Okri's book *The Freedom Artist* there is a very moving scene. The book is set in a dystopian society where people have been imprisoned and lost. A child enters the prison, and the prison is destroyed, and the child leads out the captives:

> Out of the prison, behind the boy, came a great procession of those who had disappeared into the endless dark. Like the creatures saved on a fabled ark, they poured forth from the immense prison. They poured out onto the tempered earth. They came out of the prison like ghosts. There were so many.

No one knew that so many had been lost in the dark. They poured out like shadows and when they came out into the air they acquired substance again.[6]

This is hope, the way of the Cross. But this book has been about the way the Church of England has used power over others – the way of the Crown. Years ago I had an anguished conversation with a white and implacable bishop (who has now left). I was pouring my heart out to my father in Christ, describing a difficult ministry situation. I could tell he was not hearing me so I mustered my courage and said that if I did not get help, I could not continue in such an intolerable situation. The conversation was over the phone, and his words burned my ears as molten lava poured in. He said, 'We do not like to have a gun put to our heads.' He referred to himself as 'We'. I was crushed. This is the Crown version of *Ubuntu*, 'I am because we are', where the 'we' is another name for the predator. I exist because he exists, and without him I am deemed to be nothing.

A criticism of the Truth and Reconciliation Commission is that there was a re-traumatising of the victims. There was a premature expectation that forgiveness would swiftly follow. Surely this moved the conversation from racial justice to race relations, stripping out the political and power dimensions.[7]

> The TRC failed to adequately address the injustices of apartheid as a legalised system of oppression which had blighted the everyday lives of many millions of South Africans.[8]

Victim support groups reported:

> these victims feel as if they are being asked to do the hard work of retrieving and recounting painful memories for the benefit of others.[9]

One of the victim support workers quotes one lady, a 'Mrs H.':

> I tell my story to the TRC ... and still I have nothing. I am so frustrated. Why do they want to know my story if they don't

do anything for me, they give me nothing except, oh, we are so sorry, Mrs H. No I will not tell my story again. They are just laughing at me.[10]

Ghost Ship

Picture a sailing ship with all those heroes, elders and ancestors who have been part of this movement for positive change. See the pride and the purpose glinting in our eyes. The waves are high, but our hope is higher. We have incredible energy and we people of colour work tirelessly in order to save the Church of England, for the sake of the nation and beyond to restore its vision and mission for today's world. To those in the Cross and Crown (Club) the enjoining of the people of colour goes unheeded. Our values, our vision, our voices are lost, mingled with those on the seabed. This book has been a documentation of a brave battle for acknowledged personhood, and a desired equal partnership to better society. It is a lament, a posthumous record of the starvation and the smothering of hope over many decades.

The ship has actually already sunk, and the people of colour in the Church of England are dead to the system and we know it not. We are the ghosts. We can haunt the system, but we have demonstrated we cannot heal the system, or even hurt the system. It was not designed with us in mind. If you are ignored for long enough, the social death, the isolation, and the futility of your efforts for change silence you and sentence you to a form of living exile – a being *in* the world of the Church of England but not *of* the world of the Church of England. Mrs H. of the TRC echoed the sentiments of many people of colour who heard I was writing this book when she said:

I am sick of telling my story. It makes them feel good to show that they are helping us, that things are really OK. They don't really want to change things and what good does telling our stories over and over and over do?

The crown that people of colour have known within the Church of England is the crown of thorns. My mother Elvira is among the ancestors now. Her name means hope. When people ask me for hope I think of her. I pray for the day when *Elvira*, hope, will be realised within a renewed Church of England. I sometimes catch her scent in the breeze, as I look to the distant horizon. I know I am not alone.

Her-Eyes-On

Once a seaworthy vessel, furnished and fast,
my crew played in harmony, proud sails solid mast,
then sunken, now salvaged, back to oceans deepest blue,
I the ship's captain, I the ship's crew,

Tossed across stormy waters,
fraying sails, battered boat,
night threatens suffocation,
a heavy, tight, buttoned up coat.

Froth and foam attack, clambering over the sides,
droplets a legion of pirates, growing in size,
humming a dirge as they mass at my feet.
I crawl to dry corner, as from the wailing water
I retreat ...

Now huddled under an old stained
duvet, which to my mother belonged,
her lullaby encircles me I drift away with
her song ...

I am a child again, in a glorious garden
a riot of flowers, a torrent of grace,
the sun is shining, I am rising
my fall, caught in her embrace ...

The light of that moment, illuminates
this, the storms are
strong but propel me to the new shore,

the light may be gone, yet the mother's song burns on,
I press and progress towards the horizon,
on this violent sea, knowing that I'm alive
because her-eyes-on, me.

And I know she's watching over me
and I sing because ...

BraveSlave[11]

But how can I sing when it is not easy, there is little respect, and it is not safe? The Cross and the Crown (Club) has its own version of 'the wolf and the lamb', and it is found in an Aesop's fable. This is one of the versions of that story. This is the Church of England in Crown mode and is a more familiar tale. The wolves are prowling and hope is drowning.

A stray Lamb stood drinking early one morning on the bank of a woodland stream. That very same morning a hungry Wolf came by farther up the stream, hunting for something to eat. He soon had his eyes on the Lamb ... 'How dare you paddle around in my stream and stir up all the mud!' he shouted fiercely. 'You deserve to be punished severely for your rashness!'

'But, your highness,' replied the trembling Lamb, 'do not be angry! I cannot possibly muddy the water you are drinking up there. Remember, you are upstream, and I am downstream.'

'You *do* muddy it!' retorted the Wolf savagely. 'And besides, I have heard that you told lies about me last year!'

'How could I have done so?' pleaded the Lamb. 'I wasn't born until this year.'

'If it wasn't you, it was your brother!'

'I have no brothers.'

'Well, then,' snarled the Wolf, 'it was someone in your family anyway. But no matter who it was, I do not intend to be talked out of my breakfast.' And without more words the Wolf seized the poor Lamb and carried her off to the forest.[12]

Notes

1 Archbishops' Council, Research and Statistics Department (2009), *Celebrating Diversity in the Church of England: National Parish Congregation Diversity Monitoring*, London: General Synod of the Church of England, p. 7.

2 Ibid., 1.2.6, p. 5.

3 Lewis, H. (2007), *A Church for the Future*, New York: Church Publishing, p. 70.

4 Craps, S. (2013), *Postcolonial Witnessing Trauma Out of Bounds*, London: Palgrave Macmillan, p. 45.

5 Isaiah 11.6–10.

6 Okri, B. (2019), *The Freedom Artist*, London: Head of Zeus.

7 Craps, *Trauma*, p. 45.

8 Ibid.

9 Ibid., p. 46.

10 Ibid.

11 An unpublished collection of poems.

12 Aesop (n.d.), *The Wolf and The Lamb – Fables of Aesop*. Available online at: https://fablesofaesop.com/the-wolf-and-the-lamb.html.

Epilogue:
'God Save the Queen!',
an alternative future history

And all the people gave a great shout of praise to the LORD, because the foundation of the house of the LORD was laid. But many of the older priests and Levites and family heads, who had seen the former temple, wept aloud when they saw the foundation of this temple being laid, while many others shouted for joy. No one could distinguish the sound of the shouts of joy from the sound of weeping, because the people made so much noise. And the sound was heard far away. (Ezra 3.11–13 NIV)

Laughter erupted from tear-streaked brown faces. The faithful few Anglicans of colour tumbled out of the Synod chamber. It was summer 1987, and they had established a beginning. The hard work had been worth it. Glynne Gordon-Carter, a feisty, whip-smart, West Indian woman had determined this would be driven through. This was nothing short of historic. After the Standing Committee had rejected a Commission for Black Anglican Concerns, Glynne and her intern, the recent returnee from Jamaica, 26-year-old Rose Hudson-Wilkin, had refused the mediation of the archbishops when things had gone badly. They sought advocacy with the Commission for Racial Equality. Barry Thorley and the others at the Association for Black Clergy appealed to the new black MPs in the Labour party, Diane Abbot, Paul Boateng and Bernie Grant, who were eager for a challenge. The political pressure, the media campaign which was mounting, and the interest from Princess Diana shifted the spotlight from the tiny band of troubadours, to the institution that housed them. The Standing Committee had to admit defeat. Public opinion was swaying the conversation. There was no apology but a clear, unequivocal adoption of a Commission with all the powers that would bring to usher in a season of reform. The hope in the air was palpable. Members of the Standing Committee wandered out of the Synod chamber crestfallen. These men and women sensed this was the beginning of the end. The *Faith in the City* report had been taken seriously, all the recommendations adopted, the campaign for women priests was growing in momentum. Who next might claim their right to priesthood and full inclusion? Eyes down, the disappointed shuffled away to absorb what had actually happened, and what would happen after that. The heavy-hearted walked on, ignoring the back slapping, vigorous handshaking, and small clusters of white allies gathering to congratulate the victors. The broken slunk offsite into the clammy stale Westminster air.

Whereas there were others, heroes like Kenneth Leech, a white radical priest who spoke up with and for the working classes, who approached Glynne and her colleagues saying, 'Right, now we can really get something done.' The archbishops were also in the queue to offer their praise to the group.

Just away from the action, far from his trademark ebullience, stood a black bishop, at that point the only black bishop, gently weeping. Under his breath he was whispering 'The truth will set you free, the truth will set us all free.' The man was Wilfred Wood, a West Indian powerhouse who commanded the respect of black society across the UK and the world. He was unafraid and unapologetic in his prophetic stance of holding Synod to account. The black networks he was a part of were his foundation, and he could stand on their hopes, prayers and actions. His white friends in high places formed a roof for him, shielding him from the debris of the prejudicial and dismissive attitudes of the system and the institution. His black and Asian multi-ethnic people were his floor and his walls, giving him a place to stand.

He allowed his mind to drift back through the last few years. Without fanfare, he made his way out into the refreshing, sunny, Westminster air, oblivious to the death-stares of those who credited him with destroying their precious church. A new time was coming, and had indeed come. He fell into his stride, quickening his pace when he spotted the pack of journalists, noses in the air, sniffing the winds of change. They would find him when he was ready, but now it was a time for contemplation on what had led to this moment.

Wilfred Wood had recently met a Ghanaian man called Akyaaba Addai-Sebo, who worked for the Greater London Council and organised Special Projects. Addai-Sebo had told Wilfred of his work instilling a sense of black pride in young people. He had told him how he had put together a team and had found funding to hold a special month during October to celebrate the black economic and cultural contribution to British society. They were going to call it Black History Month, and along with the new black MPs, Wilfred was invited to play a part. Wilfred would ensure that the Church of England would be among the first to adopt the initiative he and others were building, known as The *Uhuru* Ten. *Uhuru* meant liberation in Swahili, and this simple idea had the power to build a powerful coalition of the willing, the wanting, and the waiting-to-be-transformed.

The Commission for Black Anglican Concerns would be able to begin doing the necessary work. They kept the term 'black' for the political edge of the word and to encompass anyone who did not have the access to the power a whiteness ideology offered, including some white people. Wilfred and others had been overseeing a racial justice movement in the Church of England communities department. There were links with key partners in government, within the BBC, sport and the justice department. This group was producing reports and audits on racial inequality and organising sustained protest. They enabled the Church of England network to have up-to-date facts and figures on racial injustice, and suggestions of how best to respond. The group amassed the resources for the church to play its full part with its partners in tackling racial injustice on the news, through radio and in the papers, in the ballot box, in local councils and on the streets when necessary. A number of black and brown women and men were attracted to join the Church of England as clergy, simply to be a part of this department of prophetic witness. The group of commentators were not always popular with the strands of the Church of England that still preferred a more gradual generational approach to change, if they endorsed change at all. The marginalised, around the edges of church, most celebrated this news. The church of the circumference, the corners and the closets. This was good news for them. A few years later, deacon Rose Hudson-Wilkin, MP Diane Abbot, Greater London Council strategist Akyaaba Addai-Sebo, academic and activist Gus John, MP Ken Livingstone, priest Kenneth Leech, and celebrity breakfast show chef and presenter Rustie Lee, were all involved in the Church of England's Truth and Reparations enquiry. Like *Faith in the City* this was groundbreaking. It led to a number of institutions taking responsibility for the gains made through the transatlantic slave trade. There was a precedent set by the Church Commissioners to utilise a percentage of its investments and property sales. This money saved was to be distributed as small grants for new enterprise, money for scholarships and clergy enhancement, and wellbeing for black and brown people in the parishes up and down the country. It was a self-referral system. A volunteer board of predominantly black and brown Anglicans per diocese would assess the claims monthly, and distribute as they saw fit. Because of The *Uhuru* Ten initiative, Anglican Christians were travelling to Egypt and Ethiopia as well as Israel for pilgrimages and were beginning to deepen a sense of a fuller identity.

The Uhuru *Initiative*

Gather ten people of colour, or as close as you can get to that number, for ten hours over ten weeks, beginning on or around the 10th day of the 10th month. Each of the ten people takes turns to lead an activity of around an hour, but no more than two, unless agreed with the group ahead of time. The group member gets to choose an activity for the other nine, or five at the minimum. It could be a meal, it could be a walk, it could be music listened to, it could be dancing, it could be debate, it could be silence, it could be protest, it could be an invited guest speaker, it could be a game, it could be a sport, it could be storytelling, it could be a bike ride, it could be seeing a play, it could be a personality quiz, it could be wisdom sharing, it could be a good ol' singsong, it could be a film, it could be volunteering with those in need together, to name a few. The guidelines are that the activity is not cost prohibitive. Many establishments offer space for free and discounted goods for those engaged in The Uhuru Ten. Also all ideas within reason are accepted without judgement. It is inclusive and accessible. For children and vulnerable adults, this is to be appropriately supervised; and for those engaging in this through their work, they have the sign-off of the relevant line management. For those incarcerated, they need to have access to good support to enact as many of their ideas as feasible within that setting.

In time the Church of England adopted it, and ten bishops, guided by consultants, picked ten themes and activities over the ten weeks for use in and around their cathedrals. Attendance and footfall at cathedrals grew as each year busloads of people travelled to the various sites. Akyaaba Addai-Sebo had always wanted a season of black heritage and history. He stated that they used October to begin with because it was the time of harvest, also because across many parts of Africa it was the time of reconciliation when tribal leaders met to reconcile their differences.[1] Addai-Sebo shared how there was a desire among some of those who were involved in Black History Month to take it through November and up to *Kwanzaa*, which is a celebration of African culture between Christmas and New Year.

Two years later Wilfred Wood decided to take a flight back home to visit Barbados. Newmont Travel had furnished him with a discounted British Airways ticket. His ginger wine for family members was wrapped up in a towel, undetected and safely in the hold. The plane sat on the tarmac preparing for departure. Wilfred was applying his seatbelt when he noticed the corner of a small book pointing upwards, trapped in the seat tray. He yanked it free and began to read. It was a fairy tale. It told a story of a kingdom and a queen and her people. He became engrossed, fuming at how one group had taken advantage of the queen's trust. One group had claimed unjust superiority. The short story was called 'Tears and Troubadours' by Ade the Griot. The plane juddered into life and roared into flight. Wilfred got to the end of the book and snapped back in his seat, causing the drink of the person sat behind him to spill. After a swift apology he returned to the last line, 'It is said she is there to this day.' Unconsciously at first, he began to hum, then sing the British national anthem but it was for this queen, the one in chains, that Wilfred's voice lifted in petition and pride. He cleared his throat preparing to sing louder when a bony finger prodded his shoulder. It was the passenger from behind. A disembodied voice said very clearly, and directly. 'Will you please shut up? Some of us are trying to sleep here.'

Note

1 https://everygeneration.co.uk/index.php/black-british-history/bhm-black-history-month/akyaaba-addai-sebo-interview.

Afterword

It was February 2020 and General Synod was in session. There had been a private members motion put forward by the Revd Andrew Moughtin-Mumby. The air was electric as the erudite priest shared stories pertaining to the church's treatment of those of the Windrush generation. In the main, these black and brown Church of England members and British citizens suffered at the hands of the church: neglected then because of racial prejudice, and rejected now by the Home Office as a number of them were deported, or suffered the threat of deportation as their records were not kept or respected.

In addition to calling for an apology from the church and a time of lament, Andrew Moughtin-Mumby also asked for an acknowledgement of institutional racism, and an indication of a willingness to stamp it out. With steely eye and heaving chest from the exertion of his challenge, the gauntlet fell with a clang and swivelled in place. The Archbishop of Canterbury eyed it and bent to pick it up, the chamber grew quiet. His words were reported in the *Independent* newspaper: 'Personally, I am sorry and ashamed. I'm ashamed of our history and I'm ashamed of our failure.' He added: 'There is no doubt when we look at our own church that we are still deeply institutionally racist.'

It was a sobering comment, and a charged moment. It was a naming of an uncomfortable and inconvenient truth. So what next, what now? Maybe another process in another setting can help. Antjie Krog, an Afrikaner poet, journalist and writer, gives an unflinching documentation of the Truth and Reconciliation Commission in South Africa. It was made up of three committees. There was the Human Rights Violations Committee to establish what was the wrong done. The Amnesty

Committee dealt with those perpetrators seeking another chance if they confessed their part in it all. And the Reparation and Rehabilitation Committee was there on behalf of the group who suffered and survived the wrong done to them.[1]

Reconciliation is incomplete without repair. Why is it so challenging to envisage the need for repair of the damage done and ongoing damage to people of colour at the hands of the Church of England and the government? Many good white Christians will say, 'It was not my hands that crushed, my voice that scarred, or my boot that struck.' They are therefore airlifted out of the category of perpetrator. But when they are set down again, do they still find themselves within the borders of the beneficiary?

Krog describes the Ugandan academic Professor Mamdani. When speaking of Apartheid, he highlights how there were few perpetrators of the heinous actions but a lot of beneficiaries of said actions. He asks: 'Should reconciliation take place between victims and perpetrators or victims and beneficiaries?'[2]

If we extend the responsibility of stamping out racism in all its forms to those who benefit from institutional racism in the Church of England, may they no longer claim ignorance?

A month after the Revd Moughtin-Mumby had elicited an apology from the Archbishop of Canterbury, the British Home Secretary Priti Patel was issuing her own apology to the same group of people. The *Guardian* newspaper listed a number of cases where people who had come from the West Indies, who were living in England, paying taxes and working until they were erased from the ledgers, were becoming fugitives and non-persons within their own country. The newspaper led a campaign that played a role in triggering the Home Office to admit to extraordinary negligence.

The report was released during the Covid-19 news cycle. The world was at saturation point, and this vital admission went largely unnoticed, buried beneath the non-existent toilet paper. The report was damning in that the government had 'institutional ignorance and thoughtlessness towards the issue of race'.

Institutional ignorance is a key way that 'institutional racism' is expressed in the Church of England. Hidari Jingorō was the Japanese artist who reportedly carved the picture proverb above a popular shrine in seventh-century Japan. It depicts three monkeys, one covering its eyes, another its ears and the third its mouth. See no evil, hear no evil, speak no evil. It speaks of the postures we contort ourselves into to avoid encountering the reality of others. If Hidari were around today, might he be tempted to carve those monkeys above General Synod? One bishop, reflecting on his time on the Committee for Minority Ethnic Anglican Concerns, says:

> I never spoke in Synod specifically on racist matters or on behalf of CMEAC … and strong ethnic minority voices were being heard in Synod without my help. My part was to further the anti-racist and full-participation agenda by encouraging individuals, and to help in the drafting and publicizing of information and policy.[3]

As a committee member he knew how difficult it was for the token cohort of black and brown people, but he chose not to speak. He encouraged them by providing pastoral support. He engaged in some administrative actions, he gave practical support, but yet he did things *for* them, not *with* them. The strong ethnic voices may have been heard, but that does not mean they were understood. There is a note of doubt when the bishop says: 'I believe I held the confidence of CMEAC's members, and remain thankful to God for delivering me into this unlikely role.'

Black and brown people are not asking for white protectors, but they are asking for partners who see, hear and speak up for the full human flourishing of black and brown people. They are asking for partners who will fight alongside them against racism in the arena, not just cheer them on from the safety of the stadium seats: white people who speak up, listen up and look up, whether or not those people of colour are in the meetings. A white senior member of clergy, speaking about diversity and inclusion, told me that when a particular black clergy person did not attend their high-level meetings, the topic of race and ethnicity did not come up. When I asked why, he replied: 'When they are not there, it's not on the agenda.'

He went on to admit that when his white clergy colleagues got together, they never spoke about being white with its privilege and pervasive orbit. He was describing a tacit unspoken pact of the beneficiaries. In regard to real reconciliation, I turn to words recorded by Antjie Krog: 'Reconciliation will only take place ... the day whites feel offended by racism instead of feeling sorry for the blacks.'[4]

I have written what I have written. I imagine the Truth Commissions as three committees on English soil: Amnesty for Perpetrators and Beneficiaries, Reparation and Rehabilitation for Those Who are Surviving the Slings and Arrows, and an examination of Human Rights Violations to establish the truth. I predict we will have many pleading innocence, others bleeding in silence, but none who can now claim ignorance.

Notes

1 Krog, A. (1999), *Country Of My Skull*, London: Vintage, p. viii.
2 Ibid., p. 170.
3 A white bishop commenting on his role with CMEAC a couple of decades ago. I have chosen not to name him even though his words are in print. When bishops and other white senior leaders read his words I invite them to reflect on themselves, and not to scapegoat him.
4 Krog, *Skull*, p. 168.

By the rivers of Babylon, there we sat down, yea, we wept, when we remembered Zion.
We hanged our harps upon the willows in the midst thereof.
For there they that carried us away captive required of us a song; and they that wasted us required of us mirth, saying, Sing us one of the songs of Zion.
How shall we sing the Lord's song in a strange land?
(Ps. 137.1–4 KJV)

Bibliography

Aesop (n.d.), *The Wolf and The Lamb – Fables of Aesop*. Available online at: https://fablesofaesop.com/the-wolf-and-the-lamb.html.

Alibhah-Brown, Yasmin (2001), *Who do We Think We Are? Imagining the New Britain*, London: Penguin Books.

Arthur Anslyn, Captain of the Caribe Queen, who was hired by the Commission of Inquiry to dive the site after 1 August. https://en.m.wikipedia.org/wiki/Arthur_Anslyn.

AUTODIDACT 17 (2020), Dr Martin Luther King Jr: 'I fear I am integrating my people into a burning house', Amsterdamnews.com. Available online at: http://amsterdamnews.com/news/2017/jan/12/dr-martin-luther-king-jr-i-fear-i-am-integrating-m/.

Baldwin, J. (1955), *Notes of a Native Son – Stranger in the Village*, Boston: Beacon Press.

Barton, M. (2005), *Rejection, Resistance, and Resurrection*, London: Darton, Longman and Todd.

Beckford, R. (2000), 'Doing Black Theology in the UKKK', *Black Theology: An International Journal* 4: 38–60.

Bernasconi, R. (2018), 'Ottobah Cugoano's place in the history of political philosophy', in George Hull (ed.), *Debating African Philosophy: perspectives identity, decolonial ethics and comparative philosophy*, London: Routledge, p. 27.

Bhanot, K. (2020), *Decolonise, not Diversify*. Media Diversified. Available online at: https://mediadiversified.org/2015/12/30/is-diversity-is-only-for-white-people/.

Browne, Whitman T. (2013), *The Christena Disaster*, Bloomington: iUniverse.

Buchanan, Colin (2006), *Taking the Long View*, London: Church House Publishing.

Called to Act Justly: a challenge to include minority ethnic people in the life of the Church of England. Report by the Stephen Lawrence Follow-Up Staff Group April 2003, London: Church House Publishing.

Calvin, John (1536/1960) *Institutes of the Christian Religion*, Vol. 20, ed. John T. McNeill, trans. Ford Lewis Battles, Philadelphia: Westminster Press, 3.7.1–5.

Church Times (2020), Statistics on BAME priests in senior posts are 'shocking'. Available online at: www.churchtimes.co.uk/articles/ 2015/17-july/news/uk/statistics-on-bame-priests-in-senior-posts-are-shocking.

Collins, A. (2001), *Stories Behind the Best Loved Songs at Christmas*, Grand Rapids: Zondervan.

Cone, J. (1970), *A Black Theology of Liberation*, Philadelphia: Lippincott.

Copeland, M. Shawn (2010), *Enfleshing Freedom*, Minneapolis: Fortress Press.

Craps, S. (2013), *Postcolonial Witnessing*, London: Palgrave Macmillan.

Dayfoot, A. (1999), *The Shaping of the West Indian Church 1492–1962*, Barbados: The Press, University of the West Indies.

DeAngelo, R. (2019), *White Fragility*, London: Allen Lane.

Erskine, N. (1998), *Decolonizing Theology*, Eritrea: Africa World Press.

Evans, Louwanda and Moore, Wendy Leo, 'Impossible Burdens: White Institutions, Emotional Labor, and Micro-Resistance', *Social Problems*, Vol. 62, Issue 3, August 2015.

Faith in the City: A Call for Action by Church and Nation: Report of the Archbishop of Canterbury's Commission on Urban Priority Areas, Church of England, London: Church House Publishing 1985.

Fryer, P. (1984), *Staying Power: The History of Black People in Britain*. London: Pluto Press.

Gibson, Edmund, Two letters of the Lord Bishop of London (London, 1727/1729), repr. in David Humphreys, *An historical account of the incorporated Society for the Propagation of the Gospel in Foreign Parts* (London, 1730; facs. New York, 1969), pp. 265–6, as quoted in Dayfoot, A., *The Shaping of the West Indian Church 1492–1962* (Barbados: The Press, University of the West Indies).

Gilroy, P. (1983), *The Black Atlantic: Modernity and Double Consciousness*, London: Verso.

Goodison, Lorna (2018), *Redemption Ground: Essays and Adventures*, Oxford: Myriad Editions.

Goosby Smith, D. (2020), Video: Dr Jaye Goosby Smith on the Difference Between Diversity and Inclusion. Charleston CEO. Available online at: http://charlestonceo.com/video/2016/12/dr-jaye-goosby-smith-difference-between-diversity-and-inclusion/.

Gordon-Carter, G. (2013), *An Amazing Journey*, London: Church House Publishing.

Gyasi, Yaa (2016), *Homegoing*, New York: Alfred A. Knopf.

Hague, Dan (2016), 'The Trauma of racism and the distorted white imagination', in *Post Traumatic Public Theology* by Stephanie N. Areal and Shelly Rambo, Basingstoke: Palgrave Macmillan.

Henderson, Ian (1976), *A Man of Christian Action, Canon John Collins – the man and his work*, Cambridge: Lutterworth Press.

Hill, C. (1963), *West Indian Migrants and the London Churches*, London: Oxford University Press.

Hood, R. (1994), *Begrimed and Black*, Minneapolis: Fortress Press.

Isiorho, D. (2002), 'Black Theology in Urban Shadow: Combating Racism in the Church of England', *Black Theology: An International Journal* Vol. 1, no. 1: 29–48.

John, G. (2020), Academic quits C of E body over chief rabbi's Labour antisemitism comments. *Guardian*. Available online at: www.the guardian.com/world/2019/dec/03/academic-quits-c-of-e-body-over-chief-rabbis-labour-antisemitism-comments.

Keyser, Catherine (2017), *Candy Boys and Chocolate Factories: Roald Dahl, Racialization, and Global Industry*, MFS Modern Fiction Studies, Vol. 63, no. 3, pp. 403–28. Project MUSE.

Lewis, Harold T. (2007), *A Church for the Future, South Africa as the Crucible for Anglicanism in the New Century*, New York: Church Publishing Inc.

Lewis, H. (1996), *Yet With a Steady Beat*, Pennsylvania: Trinity Press International.

Lorde, Audre (2018), *The Master's Tools Will Never Dismantle the Master's House*, London: Penguin Classics.

King, Martin Luther Jr (1963), Address at the Freedom Rally, Cobo Hall, Detroit, Michigan. Stanford University, The Martin Luther King Jr Research and Education Institute.

Moss Kanter, Rosabeth (1977), *Men and Women of the Corporation*, New York: BasicBooks.

Myers, C. (2008), *Binding the Strong Man*, Maryknoll, NY: Orbis Books.

Okri, B. (2019), *The Freedom Artist*, London: Head of Zeus.

Olusoga, D. (2016), *Black and British*, London: Macmillan.

Olusoga, David (2014), *The World's War*, London: Head of Zeus.

Pilkington, A. (2003), *Racial Disadvantage and Ethnic Diversity in Britain*, Basingstoke: Palgrave Macmillan.

Pinto, R., Ashworth, M. and Jones, R. (2008), 'Schizophrenia in black Caribbeans living in the UK; an exploration of underlying causes of the high incidence rate', *British Journal of General Practice* 58 (551): 429–38.

Reddie, A. (2003), *Nobodies to Somebodies*, Peterborough: Epworth Press.

Rediker, M. (2007), *The Slave Ship*, London: John Murray Publishing.

Selby, P. (1991), *Belonging: Challenge to a Tribal Church*, London: SPCK.

Sherwood, H. (2020), Church of England appoints first black bishop in 20 years. *Guardian*. Available online at: www.theguardian.com/world/2016/dec/20/church-of-england-appoints-first-black-bishop-20-years-woyin-karowei-dorgu.

Sturrock, Donald (2010), *Storyteller*, New York: Simon and Schuster.

Talent and Calling (2007), 4.3.3: www.churchofengland.org/sites/
default/files/2018-10/gs1650-talent%20and%20calling%3A%20
a%20review%20of%20the%20law%20and%20practice%20
regarding%20.pdf.

The Church of England in Parliament (2020), Bishop of Chelmsford
responds to Government statement on race disparity audit. Available online at: https://churchinparliament.org/2017/10/10/bishop-
of-chelmsford-responds-to-government-statement-on-race-disparity-
audit/.

Washington, J. (1984), *Anti-Blackness in English Religion 1500–1800*,
New York: The Edwin Mellen Press.

Welby, J. (2018), *Reimagining Britain*, London: Bloomsbury Publishing.

Wilkinson, J. (1993), *Church in Black and White*. Edinburgh: St
Andrew's Press.

Wilkinson, John, Wilkinson, Renate and Evans Jr, James H. (1985),
'Inheritors Together: Black people in the Church of England', Race,
Pluralism and Community Group, Board for Social Responsibility of
the Church of England.

Wood, Wilfred (1994), *Keep the Faith Baby*, Oxford: The Bible Reading Fellowship.

Wood, Wilfred and Downing, John (1968), *Vicious Circle*, London:
SPCK.